HIGHLIGHT
Beginner
Student's Book

Scott Thornbury

Course consultant: Michael Vince

Heinemann English Language Teaching
A division of Heinemann Publishers (Oxford) Ltd
Halley Court, Jordan Hill, Oxford OX2 8EJ

OXFORD MADRID ATHENS PARIS FLORENCE PRAGUE
SÃO PAULO CHICAGO MELBOURNE AUCKLAND
SINGAPORE TOKYO IBADAN GABORONE JOHANNESBURG
PORTSMOUTH (NH)

ISBN 0 435 24134 6

Designed by Glynis Edwards
Picture Research by Jane Taylor
Cover illustration by David Brancaleone
Cover photography by Ben Campbell

Author acknowledgements
I would like to thank Michael Vince, the author of Highlight
Intermediate and Highlight Upper Intermediate, for his
support on this project. Thanks, too, to my colleagues at
International House, Barcelona, and many, many thanks to
Piet Luethi for the work he put in and his support overall.
Also, my thanks to my publisher, Chris Hartley, for his
constant encouragement, and to the Heinemann team in
Spain, Jane Phelps in particular, for theirs. Finally, to my
editor, Xanthe Sturt Taylor, and her unstinting dedication
to the project, I owe an incalculable debt of gratitude.

The publishers would like to thank Ruth Sanchez, Maria
Galbis, Chris Martin, and Joanne Hazapi.

The author and publishers would like to thank the following
for permission to reproduce their material. In cases where
they have been unsuccessful in contacting copyright holders
they will be pleased to make the necessary arrangements at
the first opportunity.
Mirror Syndication International for *Computers turned my boy
into a robot*, p 77; Plus Travel for advertisement, p 60;
Hoseasons for advertisement, p 60; Discover the World Ltd
for advertisement, p 60; SDA Ltd for Red Sea Holidays
advertisement, p 60; Reed Consumer Books Ltd for cartoon
from Mel Calman, p 97

Commissioned photography by Gareth Boden: pp 1, 4 (5),
8 (b), 10 (t), 16, 28, 41, 50, 108

Photo acknowledgements
Ace Photo Agency pp 25 (3 and 5), 34 (b and c), 43 (bottom),
93 (tl), 95 (tl); Anderson White Hill p 87 (d and e); Anthony
Blake Photo Library, p 39; Art Directors pp 10 (b,c,d), 51 (2),
58 (r), 71 (centre and bottom), 93 (bl); Britstock IFA pp 18,
38 (c), 93 (third top); John Birdsall Photography, p 94; Mark
Wagner, p 38 (a); Mirror Syndication International, p 77;
Orient Express Press Office p 34; Patrick Harrison p 87; Rex
Features pp 5, 11 (a and e), 12, 33, 47 (3, 4, 7), 51 (br), 93 (tr),
95 (bl), 104 (a, c and d); Robert Harding Picture Library,
pp 34 (d), 47 (2), 93 (second top and bottom, br); Science Photo
Library, p 66 (c); Sporting Pictures UK Ltd. pp 11 (c, d and e),
21; The Image Bank, p 66 (a and g), 71 (t); The Kobal Collection
p 82 (c); The Ronald Grant Archive p 82 (a, b and d); Trip pp 4,
7, 10 (a), 15, 25 (1, 2 and 3), 34 (d), 38 (c), 43 (top and centre),
51 (1, 3, 4, 6), 58, 66 (b, d, e, f), 68, 69, 103 (a, b, c, d, f); Zefa
pp 47 (1, 5, 6, 8, 9), 51 (5), 65, 93 (g), 95 (tr, br), 100.

Illustrations
Adrian Barclay pp 31, 56; Aziz Khan pp 2, 53; Clyde Pearson
pp 2, 32, 36, 49, 62, 81, 88; Diana Gold pp 19, 29; Ed McLachlan
pp 20, 25, 43; Francis Scappaticci pp 3, 27; Gillian Martin pp 14,
20, 50, 59; Jo Dennis p 9; Joan Corlass pp 10, 11, 19, 27, 40;
Maggie Ling pp 46, 48, 102; Martin Berry pp 8, 13, 37, 96;
Patrick Williams pp 4, 6, 64, 107; Peter Harper pp 61, 67;
Richard Durand p 5.

Recorded by James Richardson at Studio AVP.
Printed and bound in Spain by Mateu Cromo

95 96 97 98 10 9 8 7 6 5 4 3 2 1

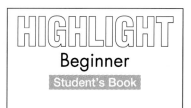

HIGHLIGHT
Beginner
Student's Book

Contents map

LISTENING	WRITING	SPEAKING	VOCABULARY	PHONOLOGY
• Listening to instructions • Letter dictation • Listening for personal information • Listening for numbers	• Writing instructions • Asking personal information	• Reading aloud	• Classroom • Prepositions of place • Action verbs • Parts of the body • Personal possessions • Numbers • Days of the week	• Letters of the alphabet
• *Biographical information*: Listening for specific information • *Shopping conversation*: Listening for prices	• Writing personal information	• Personal information: interviews • Shopping dialogues	• Personal information • Nationalities • Jobs • Consumer durables • Places in town • Numbers • Months and dates	• Contractions: *A* vs *an*
• *Personal information*: Listening for specific information • *Describing people*: Listening for gist	• Describing people	• Describing people	• Family • Daily routine • Appearance • Numbers and fractions • Irregular plurals	• Word stress
• *Transport habits*: Listening for specific information • *Timetable information*: Listening for specific information	• Writing about habits and routines	• Talking about habits and routines • Asking for timetable information	• Time expressions • Daily routine verbs • Transport *get*	• Sentence stress
• *Making a shopping list*: Listening for specific information • *Ordering a pizza*: Listening for specific information	• Writing an informal invitation	• Making requests and invitations	• Food and drink • Containers • Metric quantities	• /ð/, /s/, /z/
• *Computer dating*: Listening for specific information • *Job interviews*: Listening for gist and specific information	• Writing a job application	• Interview: likes and dislikes	• Leisure activities • Languages • Types of music	• *Can* vs *can't*

LISTENING	WRITING	SPEAKING	VOCABULARY	PHONOLOGY
• *Holiday journeys*: Listening for gist and for specific information • *Holiday plans*: Listening for gist	• Writing a simple holiday postcard	• Describing journeys • Talking about travel plans	• Holidays and travel • go + *ing*	• Weak forms: schwa
• *Describing houses*: Listening for specific information • *Comparing houses*: Listening for specific information	• Writing a description of a house or flat	• Phoning about a flat	• Housing • Furniture • Adjectives of description	• Contrastive sentence stress
• *Radio phone-in*: Listening for gist • *Following directions*: Listening for gist	• Writing a film review	• Giving advice • Making recommendations	• Geography • Action verbs • Prepositions of movement • Journeys	• Sound-spelling relationships
• *Shopping conversations*: Listening for gist • *Giving directions*: Intensive listening	• Writing directions	• Asking for information • Shopping	• Shops and amenities • Two-part verbs • Compound nouns	• Intonation: key
• *Meeting for the first time*: Listening for gist • *Invitations*: Listening for specific information	• Describing yourself	• Conversational gambits • Meeting and inviting	• Character and appearance • Adjectives • Nationalities • Negative prefixes	• Word linking: contractions
• *Accident stories*: Listening for gist • *Shopping exchanges*: Listening for gist	• Writing about an accident	• Doctor – patient role play • Narrating	• Illnesses • Adjectives of sensation • Verbs of accident • Parts of the body • Irregular plurals	• Rhythm

Unit 1 Don't Write!

1 Match the words.

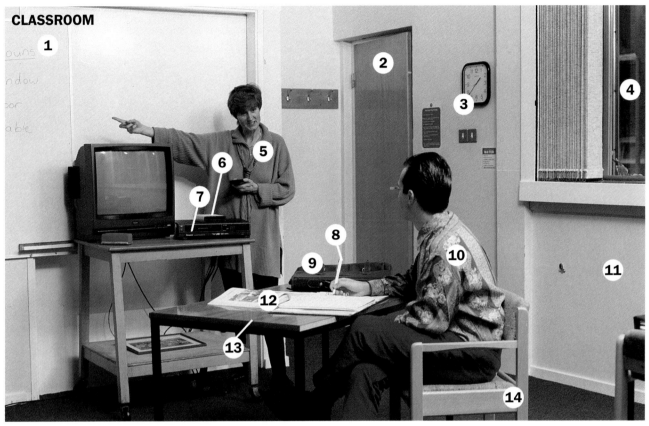

CLASSROOM

a video	**f** book	**k** clock
b cassette	**g** pen	**l** window
c board	**h** teacher	**m** door
d chair	**i** student	**n** wall
e table	**j** bag	

2 Listen to the teacher.

Point to the window.

LANGUAGE ACTIVITIES

▶ Imperatives
▶ Prepositions of place
▶ Verb *to be*
▶ Alphabet
▶ Numbers

1 Listen to the teacher.

Imperatives ▶ 1
Stand up.
Don't sit down.
Point to the window.

2 Tell another student.

Walk to the door.

3 Play this game. Watch the teacher. Listen to the teacher.

Touch your leg.
Don't sit down.

4 Match the words with the pictures.

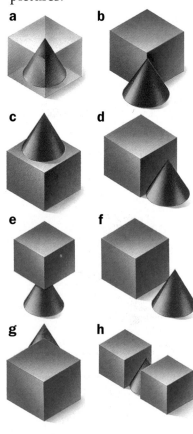

on	in
next to	behind
near	in front of
under	between

Prepositions of place ▶ 38
The book is **under** the table.
The clock is **on** the wall.

5 Listen to the teacher.

Put the book on the table.

6 Ask questions.

Where is the book?
It's under the table.

Verb *to be* ▶ 2
Where **is** the clock?
It'**s** on the wall.

7 What's the difference?
Talk to another student.

In picture 2 the chair is on the table.

8 Say these numbers and letters.

1 2 3 4
5 6 7 8 9 10
a b c d e f g h
i j l k l m n o p
q r s t u v
w x y z

9 Spell your name. Say your telephone number.

10 Follow these instructions.

Turn to the front of the book.
Find the Contents Map.
Where is Unit 2?

It's on page …

Where is Unit 5?
Where is Unit 12?
Where is 'can (ability)'?
Where is 'present perfect'?

Turn to the back of the book.
Where is the Grammar Reference?
Find 'Imperatives'.
Where is the index?
Find 'Giving instructions'.

SKILLS: READING AND LISTENING

Pre-reading

1 Match the words and signs.

a Go.
b Don't talk.
c Go in.
d Stop.
e Don't smoke.

 1    **2**    **3**

 **4**    **SILENCE 5**

Reading

2 Put in the missing words.

What's your name?   Good morning.
Stand up.   Read the letters.
Question: What's Tony's problem? His ears? His eyes? His teeth?

Speaking

3 Practise the conversation.

Pre-listening

E I
O A U
N T D S L
C R M K V Z J B
W F P G M Y H X Q

4 Say the letters.

5 Listen to the teacher.
Listen to other students.

Listening

6 At the Doctor's. Listen and complete.

Name: _____
Age: _____
Telephone: _____
Medical History:

7 Listen again, and write the questions.

_____ name?
____ old _____?
_____ phone _____?

Speaking

8 Ask other students.

Name: _____
Age: _____
Telephone: _____

The body

1 Label the parts of the body.

Imperatives ▶ 1

2 Make eight sentences.

(Don't)	point to	the	book
	touch		bag
	walk to		clock
			pen
			window
			video
			door
			teacher
		your	head
			eyes
			toes
			nose

Prepositions ▶ 38

3 Make eight sentences.

One ear is next to the nose.

5

Verb *to be* ▸ 2

4 Make questions.

Where's the bag?   It's under the table.
It's on the wall.
The teacher's in the classroom.
He's in the hospital.
It's on page 26.
It's at the back of the book.

5 Write 6 questions and answers about your classroom.

Where's the board?   *It's on the wall.*

6 Complete the conversation.

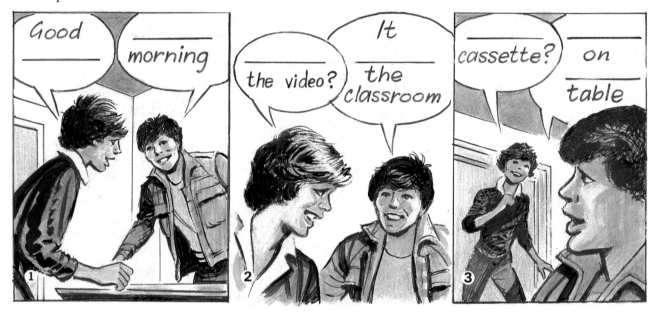

Numbers

7 Answer the questions.

   a What's four and three?   *Seven.*
   b What's seven minus three?   *Four.*
   c What's eight and one?
   d What's three and three?
   e What's nine minus four?
   f What's ten and six?
   g What's twenty minus nine?
   h What's seven and five?
   i What's eight and eight?
   j What's fourteen minus one?
   k What's twenty-two minus five?
   l What's twelve and eleven?

Pre-listening

1 What are these sports?

a

b

c

2 🔊 Listen and complete the results.

Toronto 2   California ____
____ ____   Baltimore ____
Kansas City ____ _____ ____
France – South Africa 6 – 4, ____, ____
_____ – _____ 6 – 4, ____, ____, ____ •
Scotland – Wales, ____
_____ – New Zealand, ____

Pre-writing

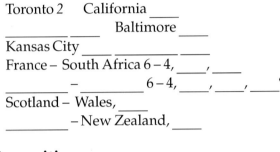

a

b

d

c

Writing

4 Write some instructions for another student.

Put your book in your bag.
Put your hands on the desk.
Stand up …

Exchange your instructions and do the actions.

3 Read and match.

1 Sit down. Put your hands behind your head. Cross your legs.
2 Sit down. Put your hands on your head. Cross your legs.
3 Lie down. Put your arms on the floor. Put your legs in the air.
4 Stand up. Put your hands on the floor between your legs.

Check your grammar
Imperatives

1 Make negative imperatives.

> No smoking = *Don't smoke.*

a No singing =
b No writing =
c No talking =
d No playing football =
e No walking =

Verb *to be*

2 Complete by adding 'is'.

.The bag under the table.
The bag is under the table.

a Jean in the classroom.
b Where Anna?
c My telephone number 268 3652.
d The board on the wall.
e What your name?
f Where the book?
g It on the table.

Build your Vocabulary
What's in your bag?

1 What are these? Use a dictionary.

Numbers

2 Write the numbers in words.

1 = *one*	11	21
2	12	22
3	13	
4	14	
5	15	
6	16	
7	17	
8	18	
9	19	
10	20	

Days

3 Put the days in order.

Monday
Saturday
Wednesday
Sunday
Tuesday
Friday
Thursday

What's today?
What's tomorrow?

Practise your pronunciation
Letters of the alphabet

1 🔲 Listen and write.

2 Spell and write.

Spell 'classroom.'

What's in *your* bag?
Make a list.

Address book

Unit 2 They're Canadian

Countries

1 What flag is it?

a

b

c

d

e

f

g

h

i

j

k

l

France Switzerland Canada
USA   Italy
Japan Hungary Germany
Spain Brazil UK Greece

Colours

2 What colour is it? Listen and guess.

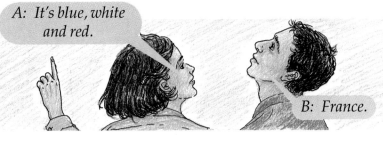

A: *It's blue, white and red.*

B: *France.*

3 Describe the flag of your country.

4 Design a flag for your class. Draw it. Write a description.

LANGUAGE ACTIVITIES

- ► Verb *to be*
- ► *A/an*
- ► Plural nouns
- ► Subject pronouns
- ► Adjectives

1 Ask and answer.

What is it?
It's a TV.
Is it Japanese?
No, it's Korean, I think.

a

b

c

d

Nationalities ► 32
It's **Korean**.

2 Show and tell.

Adjectives ► 31
It's **cheap**.
It's a **Swiss** watch.

Is it new?   *Is it a good watch?*

Is it a Swiss watch?   *Is it cheap or expensive?*

3 Make sentences about David and Julia.

David is a fireman.

A/an ► 20
David is **a** fireman.
Are you **an** actor?

4 What are the questions?

What do you do, David?

Verb *to be* ► 2
Are you married?
Where **is** she from?
I'**m** 19.

I'm a fireman.

Canadian.

30.

Yes, I'm married.

In Ontario.

5 Ask other students. Complete this form.

	1	2	3	4	5	6
NAME:						
NATIONALITY:						
ADDRESS:						
AGE:						
OCCUPATION:						
MARRIED/SINGLE:						

6 Report your information.

Odile is from France.
She's a student.
She's 19 …

Role play

7 You are one of these people. Introduce yourself to two other students.

Hello, I'm … I'm from …

8 Think of a famous person. Can the other students guess?

Are you American? Are you an actor? …

a

b

c

d

e

f

SKILLS: READING AND LISTENING

Pre-reading

1 What are their real names?
Match the old name with the new name.

Old Name	New Name
Georgios Panaylotou	Elton John
Thomas Mapother	Tina Turner
Caryn Johnson	George Michael
Cherilyn Sarkisian	Tom Cruise
Reginald Dwight	Whoopee Goldberg
Anna Mae Bullock	Bruce Lee
Lee Yuen Kam	Cher

Reading

2 Read and answer the questions.

FACT FILE

Tina Turner

Original name:	Anna Mae Bullock
Date of birth:	26/11/39
Born:	Nutbush, Tennessee, USA
Lives:	London and Paris
Marital Status:	Divorced
Eyes:	Brown
Height:	1.73m
Weight:	57.3kg
Car:	Mercedes Jeep
First Hit:	"*Let's stay together*" (November 1983)
Biggest Hit:	"*What's Love Got To Do With It*" which reached Number Two in Britain in June 1984. It sold more than 750,000 copies.

FACT! She starred in the film "*Mad Max 2 (Beyond Thunderdome)*" with Mel Gibson.

FACT! In the Sixties Tina had lots of hits with her husband Ike, but they divorced in 1976.

FACT! A film about her life, called "*What's Love Got To Do With It*" was released in 1993.

a What is Tina Turner's real name?   *Anna Mae Bullock*
b Was she born in the USA?
c When's her birthday?
d Where does she live?
e Is she married?
f What colour are her eyes?
g How much does she weigh?
h What was her first hit?
i How many copies were sold of 'What's Love Got To Do With It'?
j What was her husband's name?
k Who starred with Tina Turner in 'Mad Max 2 (Beyond Thunderdome)'?
l What was the name of the film about her life?

Pre-listening

3 Match the questions with the answers:

How old are you?	January 14th.
Where do you live?	No, I'm single.
What's your first name?	I'm a librarian.
What's your full name?	I'm English.
Where are you from?	Christine.
Are you married?	In Cambridge.
When's your birthday?	Christine Morgan.
What do you do?	26.

Listening

4 🎧 Listen and complete.

FULL NAME: *Vikram Seth*

AGE:

NATIONALITY:

OCCUPATION:

DATE OF BIRTH:

MARITAL STATUS:

ADDRESS:

Speaking

5 Interview another student. Report to the class.

How old are you?

She's 22.

Nationalities ▶ 32

1 What are the nationalities? Put the adjectives into three groups:

Italy	Russia	Spain
Portugal	Canada	Sweden
China	Brazil	Japan
England	Hungary	Egypt
Ireland	Australia	Turkey

-ian	-ese	-ish

Italian

2 Make sentences.

a He's from Italy. *He's Italian.*
b I'm from Turkey. *I'm*
c She's from Ireland.
d They're from Portugal.
e You're from Hungary.
f Ahmed's from Egypt.
g Kazuo and Yukio are from Japan.

Jobs

3 Match the job with the place.

doctor	office
teacher	shop
actor	library
secretary	bank
sales assistant	hospital
mechanic	university
librarian	theatre
professor	school
bank clerk	garage

4 Make sentences.

A doctor works in a hospital.

a A teacher _____
b An actor _____
c _____ in a university.
d _____ in an office.
e A bank clerk _____
f _____ in a library.
g A mechanic _____
h _____ in a shop.

Adjectives ▶ 31

5 Make 5 sentences and 5 questions from this table.

It's	a	red	book	
Is it	an	old	watch	
		new	motor-scooter	?
		expensive	video	
		cheap	car	
		Japanese	computer	
		English	dictionary	

6 Complete these questions with *do, are, is*.

a How old ____ you?
b Where ____ you live?
c What ____ your name?
d Where ____ you from?
e ____ you married?
f When ____ your birthday?
g What ____ you do?
h Where ____ you work?

7 Write the questions.

A: Hello.
B: Hello.
A: (1) Where _____?
B: I'm from Latvia.
A: (2) Where _____?
B: Latvia is near Russia.
A: (3) What _____?
B: I'm a student.
A: (4) How _____?
B: I'm 19.
A: (5) What _____?
B: Yelena.
A: (6) Are _____?
B: No, I'm single.
A: (7) Where _____?
B: I live in Riga, the capital of Latvia.

Verb *to be* ▶ 2

8 Make sentences about Paulo and Rosa.

Paulo is Portuguese.
He's ...

FULL NAME: Paulo Futre
NATIONALITY: Portuguese
OCCUPATION: football player
AGE: 21
MARITAL STATUS: single

Rosa is ...

FULL NAME: Rosa Siza
NATIONALITY: Portuguese
OCCUPATION: social worker
AGE: 21
MARITAL STATUS: married

9 Interview Paulo.

What's your full name?
Paulo Futre.

I'm Portuguese.
I'm a football player.
I'm 21.
No, I'm single.

10 Interview Rosa. Write the questions and answers.

What's your full name?

11 Write four sentences about yourself.

Pre-listening

1 How much is it?

Listening

2 🔊 Listen and write the prices.

the dictionary
the blue pen
the black pen
the cassettes
the batteries

3 Listen again, and complete.

a Good morning.
Good morning. Can I help you?
Yes, I _____ a dictionary.
An _____ dictionary?
A _____ -English dictionary.
This one is _____.
OK. I'll _____ it.

b Yes, can I _____ you?
Yes, _____ a pen.
Blue _____ black?
How much _____ the blue pen?
_____ dollar.
And the black one?
_____ .
_____ _____ the blue one.

c Good afternoon.
Good _____.
How much _____ the cassettes?
Three for _____.
_____ six, then.
That's $10.00.

Speaking

4 Student A: You are a sales assistant.
Student B: You are a customer.
Practise the conversation.

Good _____.
Good _____.
Can I _____?
Yes. I _____ a notebook. How much _____ the red notebook?
£ _____
How _____ blue _____?
£ _____
I'll take the _____.
That's _____.
Thank you.
Thank you.

Writing

5 Write about yourself. Include this information:

Name, age, nationality, occupation, marital status, birthday, address and telephone number.

My name's ...

Check your grammar

Verb *to be*

1 Complete with *is, am, are.*

   a I ___ Egyptian.
   b She ___ French.
   c They ___ Italian.
   d ___ you Swedish?
   e ___ he Spanish?
   f ___ it a Japanese car?

2 Write the negatives.

   a I*'m not* Egyptian.
   b She _____ French.
   c They _____ Italian.
   d You _____ Swedish.
   e He _____ Spanish.
   f It _____ a Japanese car.

Adjectives

3 Correct or not?

   a It's a car green.
   b How much are the reds pens?
   c Is your watch new? No, it's old.
   d They are students Italians.
   e Angel's a Spanish teacher.

Build your Vocabulary

Numbers 20–100

1 Write the numbers in words.

20 = *twenty*	52 =
21 =	60 =
25 =	70 =
30 =	80 =
33 =	90 =
40 =	99 =
50 =	100 =

Months

2 What's the first month?
January.

   What's the second month?
   What's the third month?
   The fourth month?
   The fifth?
   The sixth?
   The seventh?
   The eighth?
   The ninth?
   The tenth?
   The eleventh?
   The twelfth?

Dates

3 1st January = *the first of January.*
   2nd January =
   3rd Jan =
   4/1 = *the fourth (4th) of January*
   5/2 =
   10/6 =
   12/4 =
   20/12 = *the twentieth of December*
   30/5 =
   21/7 =

   When's your birthday?

Practise your pronunciation

Contractions

1 What's the contraction?
Re-write the sentence with the contraction. Read each sentence aloud.

What is your name?
What's your name?

   a It is a Japanese radio.
   b He is American.
   c Maria is Portuguese.
   d When is your birthday?
   e What is your job?
   f They are both 21.
   g I am Australian.
   h What is your address?
   i It is £5.00.

A/an

2 *A* or *an*?

   a It's ___ new watch.
   b It's ___ old watch.
   c She's ___ doctor.
   d He's ___ actor.
   e She works in ___ office.
   f They work in ___ university.
   g Is it ___ expensive dictionary?

3 ▭ Listen and repeat.

STARTING POINTS

1 Look at this family. What are the relationships?

grandmother
grandfather
father
mother
wife
husband
sister
brother
son
daughter
uncle
aunt
children
parents
cousins

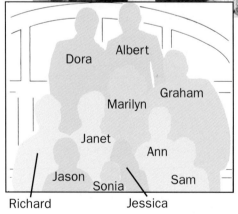

Dora
Albert
Graham
Marilyn
Janet
Ann
Jason
Sonia
Sam
Richard
Jessica

2 Fill in the family tree.

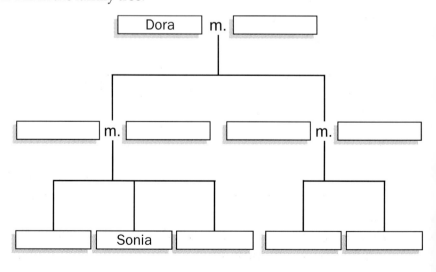

3 Draw your family tree. Tell another student.

LANGUAGE ACTIVITIES

▶ Verb *to be*, singular and plural
▶ Possessive adjectives
▶ *Have*
▶ *Any*
▶ Possessive *'s*
▶ Present simple, 3rd person singular

1 Read and answer.

Hello. My name's Janet and I'm a secondary school teacher. I live with my husband Ricard in Lille, in the north of France. Ricard is a librarian and he works at the University of Lille. We have three children, Jessica, Jason and Sonia. Jessica and Jason are twins and are both six. Sonia is one. I have one brother, Graham, and he is married. His wife's name is Marilyn. She's Australian. They live in Australia. They have a son, Sam, and a daughter, Ann. Graham is an architect and Marilyn is a housewife.

a What does Janet do?
b Where does she live?
c Where does Ricard work?
d How many children do they have?
e How old is Jessica?
f What's Graham's wife's name?
g What does Marilyn do?

2 Write more questions about the text and ask another student. Can they remember?

Present simple ▶ 5
I **live** in Reading.
Where **does** Richard **work**?
How many children do they **have**?

***Have* ▶ 3**
We **have** three children.
How many children do they **have**?

***Any* ▶ 24**
Do they have **any** children?

3 Who works where?

in a library
in an office
at home
in a school

Who lives where?

Where do *you* work? Where do *you* live?

4 Make a questionnaire. Ask other students.

where / live?
where / work?
brothers and sisters?
children?
how old?

5 Write a report.

Paola has two brothers, Umberto and Tomaso. Umberto is 21. He is a student. Tomaso...

6 True or false?
Janet is a housewife.   *False*
Richard lives in Australia.
True

Write sentences about yourself. Some are true, some are false. Read your sentences to other students. Can they guess which are true, and which are false?

7 True or false? What do you think?

> That's true.

> That's not true. Not all Italians drink coffee.

In England they drive on the left. They don't drive on the right.
Italians drink coffee. They don't drink tea.
Australians wear shorts. They don't wear long trousers.
In the USA they drive big cars. They don't drive small cars.
The Japanese eat fish. They don't eat meat.
In Australia they play cricket. They don't play baseball.
In the USA they play baseball. They don't play football.

Write some facts. Are they true or false?
In India they …
The French …

> **Present simple ▶ 5**
> They **drink** tea.
> They **don't drink** coffee.

8 Find someone in your group who …
drinks tea
doesn't eat meat
has three brothers
works in an office
drives a big car
plays football
…
…
…

Do you eat meat?

Report to the class.
Jean-Paul doesn't eat meat …

Role play

9

> **Room** in flat for one person or a couple. N o n - s m o k e r s. $120 a month.

A: You have a room in your flat. You want someone to live in it. Interview B.
B: You want a room in a flat. Answer A's questions.

A: *How old are you?*
Are you married?
Do you have any children?
Do you smoke?

Pre-reading

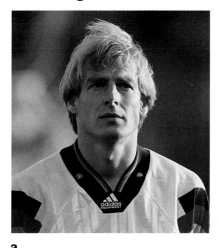
a

b

c

1 What is the same about these people?

Reading

2 Read this interview with Arantxa Sanchez Vicario. Match the
questions with the answers.

What was your first big success?
Tell me about your family.
What do you do when you're not playing tennis?
Tell me a bit about yourself.

I was born in Barcelona in December 1971. My father's
family name is Sanchez and my mother's family name is
Vicario.I use my mother's family name because she helped
me so much.

My sister Marisa and my brother Emilio are both tennis
players.We all started playing tennis when we were very
young. Marisa now lives in the United States.I live with my
parents in Barcelona.

That was in Granada. I became Spanish champion. I was
only 13. My brother won the men's championship at the
same time. Five months later I started playing
professionally.

I like listening to music. I like the Beatles, Phil Collins, and Bruce Springsteen. I like
playing cards when I travel. I have a dog, too. His name is Roland, named after the Roland
Garros Tournament in Paris, which I won in 1989, and again in 1994.

3 Now complete the information.

Name: ....
Nationality: ....
Occupation: ....
Age: ....
Lives: ....
Brothers and sisters: ....
Parents: ....

4 Make questions about the other people in Activity 1.

What does she do?

5 How many questions can you answer?

Listening

6 ⌨ Listen to these people talking about themselves and fill in the grid.

	Name	Age	Job	Marital status	Children	Family	Home
1	James						
2							
3							
4							

Writing

7 Use the information in the grid to write about one of the people.

James is a student. He is 19. He studies art and design at the Royal College of Art. He has a girlfriend, Andrea. They live in London. James has two sisters, Natasha and Lara. His parents are divorced.

Speaking

8 Who is your best friend? Tell another student.

Frank is my best friend. He's a … He lives in …

GRAMMAR AND VOCABULARY

Verbs

1 Match the verbs with the nouns.

read   a sandwich
drink   trousers
drive   a book
write   coffee
watch   Japanese
eat   television
play   a letter
listen to   a car
study   football
wear   a cigarette
smoke   the radio

2 Use these verbs to complete the sentences.

drink   eat   work   drive
play   live   wear   have
write

a I don't _____ meat but I _____ fish.
b Do you _____ tennis?
c Where does Graham _____? In an office.
d Do the Japanese _____ tea or coffee?
e I _____ in Reading but I work in London.
f In Japan they _____ kimonos.
g Do you _____ to your parents?
h They _____ three children.
i They have a car, but they don't _____ to the office.

Verb *to be*, singular and plural ▶ 2

3 Complete the text with *is, are, am*.

My name ____ Graham and I ____ an architect. I live in Australia with my wife, Marilyn. I ____ English but Marilyn ____ Australian. We have one son, Sam. He ____ twelve. My sister, Janet, lives in France. She ____ married to Ricard. Their twins, Jessica and Jason, ____ six and their daughter Sonia ____ one and a half. My parents ____ both English.

4 Write the questions.

A: _____?
B: I'm from Viet Nam.
A: _____?
B: I'm a taxi driver.
A: _____?
B: No, I'm single.
A: _____?
B: I'm 27.

A: _____?
B: Yes. One sister and two brothers.
A: _____?
B: She's 31.
A: _____?
B: Yes, she's married.

Have ▶ 3

5 Look at this family tree. Write sentences with *have* in the correct form.

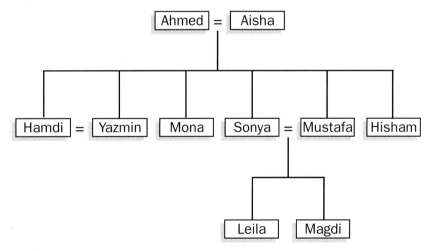

a Ahmed and Aisha *have* four children.
b Hamdi _____ two sisters and a brother.
c Mona _____ two brothers and a sister.
d Sonya and Mustafa _____ two children.
e Hamdi and Yazmin _____ any children.
f Leila _____ one brother.
g Leila _____ any sisters.
h Ahmed and Aisha _____ two grandchildren.

6 Write the questions for Activity 5.

    a *How many children do Ahmed and Aisha have?*

Any ▶ 24

7 Complete with *one, two, or any*.

    a Ahmed: 'I have ____ daughters.'
    b Yazmin: 'I don't have ____ children.'
    c Magdi: 'I don't have ____ brothers.'
    d Leila: 'I have ____ brother.'
    e Mona: 'I have ____ brothers.'
    f 'Hamdi, do you have ____ children?'
    g Ahmed has ____ grandchildren.

Possessive '*s* ▶ 36

8 You are Hamdi. Describe your family.

    My name is Hamdi. My father's name is Ahmed. My mother's …

Possessive adjectives ▶ 35

9 Complete using *his, her, your, their*.

    a My brother is a doctor.
       Oh? What's *his* name?
    b My mother is an architect.
       Oh? What's _____ name?
    c I've got two brothers.
       Oh? What are _____ names?
    d I'm a new student.
       Oh? What's _____ name?
    e My father is a teacher.
       Oh? What is _____ name?
    f My sisters are twins.
       Oh? What are _____ names?
    g My grandmother is 99.
       Oh? What's _____ name?

Present simple ▶ 5

10 Complete with these verbs:

    work works live lives
    have has study studies

    Alan: I live in Halifax, Canada. I ____ with my family. My parents are both social workers. They ____ in Halifax. I'm a student – I ____ economics. My girlfriend's name is Patricia. She's a student too. She ____ German and French. Patricia ____ near Halifax. She ____ one brother, Tom. Tom is a teacher. He ____ in a school in Halifax. He's married to Diane. Tom and Diane ____ three children.

11 Make 6 questions and answers about Alan.

    Where does he live?
    He lives in Halifax.

12 Write about yourself.

    Where do you live? What do you do? Have you got any brothers and sisters? What do they do? …

SKILLS: LISTENING AND WRITING

Pre-listening

1 Which adjectives go with these pictures?

a   b   c   d

tall   short
dark   fair
old   young
good-looking   not very good-looking
bright   not very bright

Listening

1   2   3   4   5

2 📼 Listen and look at the pictures. Who is who? (There are five people and four descriptions).

3 Listen and write the exact words.

My brother _____ .

_____

I think _____ .

_____

He's tall _____

_____

He's very athletic – _____

_____

Speaking

4 Describe one of the people in Activity 2. Can other students guess who it is?

Writing

5 Write a description of the fifth picture.

He's ...

3

Check your grammar
Possessive adjectives

1 Complete this table.

Subject	Possessive
I	my
you	
	her
he	
we	our
they	

Verb *to be*

2 Complete with *is, are, am*.

a How old ____ she?
b I ____ from Australia.
c ____ you married?
d Jessica and Jason ____ twins.
e Where ____ the school?
f ____ Arantxa Spanish?

Have

3 Complete with *have* or *has*.

a They ____ four children.
b Evelyn ____ a boyfriend.
c I ____ a new video.
d Do you ____ any brothers and sisters?
e What does he ____ in his bag?
f I don't ____ any children.
g Does Alan ____ a job?
h Ricard ____ a Japanese car.

Build your Vocabulary
Numbers

1 What are these numbers? Write the words.

a 2 ½ = *two and a half*
b 3 ¼
c 12 ½
d 50% = *fifty per cent*
e 90%
f 1 ¾
g 8 ½
h 20%

Plurals

2 What are the plurals?

brother = *brothers*
parent =
son =
baby =
child =
man =
woman =
grandchild =

3 Write the plural.

My son is very bright.
= *My sons are very bright.*

a Her uncle is old.
b Their child is not very good-looking.
c My book is red. Your book is blue.
d He is a new student.
e The fair man is my brother.

Practise your pronunciation
Word stress

1 📼 Listen and mark the stress.

January	July
February	August
March	September
April	October
May	November
June	December

2 How many syllables in these words? Where is the stress? Listen and check.

doctor = *2 syllables. Stress on first syllable.*

teacher
actor
student
driver
housewife
assistant
mechanic
professor
architect
librarian
secretary

Unit 4 When?

STARTING POINTS

1 Match the time with the clock.

one o'clock
half past three
quarter past seven
quarter to ten
ten past six
twenty to eleven

2 Draw six clocks and listen to the teacher.

3 Draw six clocks and listen to another student say different times.

4 Practise the dialogue.

Excuse me?

Yes?

What's the time?

It's _____.

Thanks.

- ▶ *Yes/no* questions – present, past, future
- ▶ Negatives – present simple
- ▶ Time expressions
- ▶ *When* + present simple

Time expressions ▶ 37

1 Put these expressions into three groups:

Past	Normally	Future
tomorrow		

on Saturdays

last week

next week

last night

tomorrow

tonight

yesterday

every day

in 1990

at eight o'clock this morning

next year

a year ago

last Saturday

at eight o'clock this evening

in 2001

Auxiliary verbs
Do/did/will ▶ 4
Do you watch TV every day?
Did you watch TV yesterday?
Will you watch TV tomorrow?

Yes/no questions

2 Do this questionnaire:

ARE YOU A CREATURE OF HABIT?

1 Do you watch TV every day?	*Yes/no*
2 Did you have watch TV yesterday?	*Yes/no*
3 Will you watch TV tomorrow?	*Yes/no/don't know*
4 Do you have three meals every day?	*Yes/no*
5 Did you have three meals yesterday?	*Yes/no*
6 Will you have three meals tomorrow?	*Yes/no/don't know*
7 Do you have a holiday every year?	*Yes/no*
8 Did you have a holiday last year?	*Yes/no*
9 Will you have a holiday next year?	*Yes/no/don't know*
10 Do you go shopping every week?	*Yes/no*
11 Did you go shopping last week?	*Yes/no*
12 Will you go shopping next week?	*Yes/no/don't know*
13 Do you brush your teeth every day?	*Yes/no*
14 Did you brush your teeth yesterday?	*Yes/no*
15 Will you brush your teeeth tomorrow?	*Yes/no/don't know*

Your score:
If you answered YES to 12–15 questions you are a creature of HABIT. Your life is one long routine. You are very reliable, but not very exciting.

If you answered NO or DON'T KNOW to 12-15 questions you are WILD and UNPREDICTABLE. You are very interesting but you're not a reliable friend.

If not – then you have a good balance between habit and excitement.

3 You can now ask questions in the past, present and future. Write more questions and ask other students.

Present simple – negatives ▶ 5

4 Who does these things in your home? You? Your father? Your mother? Your husband? Your wife? Your brothers and sisters? Your children?

Who cooks?
Who goes shopping?
Who cleans the house?
Who looks after the children?
Who takes the children to school?
Who drives?
Who answers the telephone?
Who earns money?

Ask other students.

5 Report.

My father goes shopping.
My sister doesn't cook.

> **Present simple: negative**
> **▶ 5**
> My sister **doesn't cook.**
> I **don't eat** meat.

When + present simple ▶ 30

6 When do you do these things?

– get up
– have breakfast
– go to work/school
– go shopping
– come home from work/ school
– have dinner
– do your homework
– watch TV
– go to bed

Ask other students.

> ***Wh* questions ▶ 30**
> **When** do you have breakfast?
> **When** did you get up?

Game

7 Ask another student about yesterday/last Sunday/last night. You get one point for every *yes* answer.

Did you go shopping last Sunday? No. (0 points)
Did you get up at seven o'clock yesterday? Yes. (1 point)

> ***Yes/no* questions ▶ 4**
> **Did** you **go** out?

29

Pre-reading

1 What does a good student do? Make a list.

A good student does his/her homework.

Reading

2 Read this article. Answer the questions.

THE GOOD LANGUAGE LEARNER

Are you a good language learner? A study of 1000 language students in the United States explains the difference between good language learners and bad language learners. For example:

● Good language learners *want* to learn the language. They have a good reason to learn the language.

● Good language learners find opportunites to speak the language. They talk to total strangers!

● Good language learners read and listen. They don't worry if they don't understand every word.

● Good language learners make mistakes but they don't worry. They take risks.

● Good language learners study the rules and do their homework.

● Good language learners ask questions. For example: 'What does this mean? How do you say 'thank you' in French/Russian/Chinese?'

True or false?

a Good language learners have a good reason to learn the language.
b Good language learners talk to total strangers.
c Good language learners worry if they don't understand every word.
d Good language learners don't make mistakes.
e Good language learners do their homework.
f Good language learners say 'thank you'.

Speaking

3 Are you a good language learner? Write questions and ask other students.

Do you worry about mistakes?

4 Practise these questions and answers.

How do you spell___?

I don't know.

How do you say _____ in English?
What does _____ mean?
How do you spell _____?

I don't know.
I can't remember.
I don't understand.

30

Pre-listening

5 What are the names of the different forms of transport?

Listening

6 🔊 Listen to these people and complete the chart.

Name	Job	Normal transport	Time	Transport today
Helen				
Franz				
Roberta				
Mary-Lou				

7 Listen to the interview with Roberta again and write the questions.

  a How do _____ work?
  b How long _____ take?
  c And did _____ today?

  Listen to Mary-Lou and write the answers.

  d So, how do you get to work?
  It _____ . _____ I take the bus. _____ I take a taxi.

Speaking

8 Ask other students the questions. Write the answers and report.

Neus takes the bus to work. It takes 20 minutes.

31

Times of day

1 What are the times of day?

afternoon midday night morning midnight evening

What are the prepositions? Choose from *in* or *at*.

in the afternoon

2 Use the expressions to write sentences.

    a I go to school *in the morning*.
    b I have breakfast
    c I have lunch
    d I have dinner
    e I come home
    f I do my homework
    g I watch TV
    h I go to the cinema
    i I go to bed
    j I go to sleep

Times and dates

3 Put the times and dates in words.

2.15 am   *quarter past two (or two-fifteen) in the morning.*

24/12/93   *the twenty-fourth of December, nineteen ninety-three.*

    a 2.30pm
    b 11.00am
    c 7.45pm
    d 11.15pm
    e 10/6/96
    f 18/4/79
    g 16/10/81

When + present simple ▸ 30

4 Do Activity 2 again. This time write the exact times.

   a *I go to school at 7.30am.*

5 Write the questions.

   I get up at 7.00am.   *When do you get up?*
   I have breakfast at 7.30am.
   I get to work at 8.00am
   I finish work at 5.00pm.
   I come home at 6.00pm.
   I have dinner at 8.30pm.
   I go to bed at 11.30pm.

6 Ask another student the questions and write the answers.

   Paola has breakfast at 8.00am.

Present simple: negatives ▸ 5

7 Write eight true sentences about yourself, using 'don't'.

   I don't eat meat. I don't smoke …

Yes/no questions ▸ 4

8 In groups of three or four, ask questions.

   Do you eat meat? Do you smoke? …

   Write sentences.

   Sergio and Raffaela eat meat. Paola doesn't eat meat …
   Everyone eats meat except Paola.

Past simple: *yes/no* questions ▸ 4

9 Who practises English? Ask other students questions about their use of English.

   Did you speak English yesterday?
   Did you read an English magazine last month?
   Did you listen to … ?

Pre-listening

1 Look at the timetable. Ask and answer questions.

LONDON – PARIS – VENICE			
	Arrive	Depart	Meals
Day 1 London(Victoria)	–	1115	Lunch
Day 1 Paris(Gare de L'Est)	2100	2140	Dinner
Day 2 Zurich(Flughafen)	0626	0645	Breakfast
Day 2 Buchs	0851	0910	–
Day 2 St Anton am Arlberg	1033	1036	–
Day 2 Innsbruck(Hbf)	1154	1222	Lunch
Day 2 Verona(Porta Nuova)	1629	1638	Tea
Day 2 Venice (Santa Lucia)	1810	–	–

a When does the train leave London for Venice?
b When does it arrive in Venice?
c How long does it take?
d Does it stop in Paris?

Now ask other students about the timetable.

Listening

2 🎧 Listen to these short conversations. Where are they?

a

b

c

d

3 Listen again and answer these questions.

a When does the next bus leave for Bristol?
b When does it arrive?
c When does the train to Richmond leave?
d Where does it leave from?
e When does the library open?
f When does it close?
g When does the film start?
h How long is it?

Speaking

4 Practise conversations using this information:

Oxford to Woodstock and Stratford-upon-Avon

Mondays to Saturdays	X50
	1315
OXFORD, Gloucester Green Bus Station	1321
Oxford, Woodstock Road, South Parade	1330
Yarnton, A44, Grapes	1333
Begbroke, Royal Sun	1339
Blenheim Palace, Gates	1340
WOODSTOCK, opp. Marlborough Arms	1341
Old Woodstock, Vermont Drive	1346
Wootton, Church	1351
Glympton Village	–
Glympton Turn	1356
Kiddington, Post Office	1400
Enstone, Green	1408
CHIPPING NORTON, West Street	

FROM THE DIRECTOR OF THE ADJUSTER AND SPEAKING PARTS

A FILM BY ATOM EGOYAN

Calendar

Mon-Fri 17.00, 19.00, 21.00
Sat and Sun 19.00, 21.00

ICA cinemas

Saturday trains

Oxford depart	London Paddington arrive
1115	1219
1126	1250B
1138	1312
1215	1319
1230	1354B
1238	1412
1315	1419
1326	1450B
1338	1512
1415	1519
1426	1550B

THE SILENCE OF A LOOK
IMAGES OF GUATEMALANS
PHOTOGRAPHS BY LUIS GONZALEZ PALMA

Foyer Galleries
Royal Festival Hall
Open daily 10 am – 10.30 pm
ADMISSION FREE

Writing

5 Write about a typical weekday (Monday-Friday).

On a typical weekday I get up at …

4

Check your grammar

Auxiliary verbs

1 Complete with *do/does, did, will*.

a _____ you read the newspaper every day?
b _____ you go to school yesterday?
c _____ the library open on Saturdays?
d _____ you be at home tomorrow?
e _____ the children normally take the bus?

Present simple

2 Complete this table.

I *take* the bus.
You _____ the bus.
She/he _____ the bus.
We _____ the bus.
They _____ the bus.

Negatives

3 Complete this table.

I *don't take* the bus.
You _____ the bus.
She/he _____ the bus.
We _____ the bus.
They _____ the bus.

Build your Vocabulary

Transport

1 What are the verbs?

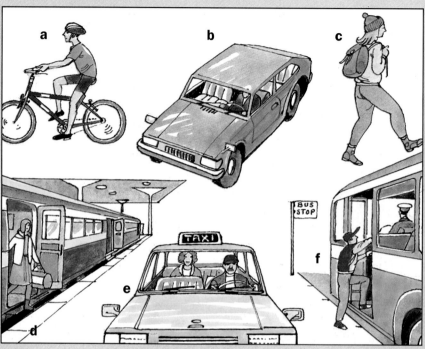

2 What one word goes in all these sentences?

a When do you _____ to work?
b When does the train _____ to Oxford?
c I _____ up at 7am every day.
d Take the train to Oxford and _____ off at Reading.
e We normally _____ home at 8 in the evening.

Practise your pronunciation

Sentence stress

1 ▭ Listen. Where is the stress?

a When does the next bus leave?
b When does the film start?
c How much does it cost?
d When does the train arrive?
e Where does it leave from?
f How long does it take?

2 Listen again and repeat.

Unit 5 What's in it?

STARTING POINTS

1 Who is saying what?

What would you like to drink? Can I help?
I'll have a coke. Can you put these on the table?
Try one of these. Can I take your coat?
What's in it? Thanks.

2 Who is eating? Who is drinking? Who is smoking? Who is
dancing? Who is cooking? Who is talking? Who is laughing?

3 Can you find these things?

food drinks glasses bottles plates
knives forks cups ice

LANGUAGE ACTIVITIES

- ► *Can…?* (requests)
- ► *Which?*
- ► *This/that; these/those*
- ► Present continuous
- ► *Would you like a…?*
- ► *A/some*
- ► *How much/how many?*
- ► *(Not) a lot of*

1 Listen to the teacher.

Can you open your books please?
Can you bring me the pen please?

Can…? (requests) ► 12
Can you say that again?
Can you pass me that folder, please?

---

2 Ask questions.

Which pen?
This pen or that pen?

Which ► 28
Which pen?

This/that; these/those ► 26
Can you pass me **that** folder?
This folder?

---

3 Make requests to other students and to the teacher.

Can you open the window, please?
Can you lend me that pen, please?

4 Make excuses.

Can you pass me that pen, please?
No, I'm using it.
What are you doing?
I'm writing.

Practise other conversations for

book   cup   fork   magazine

Present continuous ► 6
What **are** you **doing**?
I'**m writing**

Offers

5 What are they saying?

Would you like…?
Yes, please/ No, thanks.
How much/many …?

Offers ► 16
Would you like a drink?
Would you like some paella?

a

b

c

6 What's in it? Match the ingredients with the dish.

Salade niçoise

Paella

Moussaka

Chilli con carne

A	B	C	D
aubergines	olives	tomatoes	beans
lamb	eggs	peppers	beef
tomatoes	tomatoes	chicken	peppers
garlic	tuna	rice	tomatoes
pepper	olive oil	prawns	onions
eggs	vinegar	mussels	garlic
cheese			chilli powder

How much?/How many? ▶ 27
How much sugar do you take?
How many sandwiches would you like?

Role play

7 Student A: Invite Student B to eat a dish from your country.
Student B: Ask questions about the dish.

8 Class survey. Find out about the eating habits of the class.

How much fruit do you eat?
How many cups of coffee do you drink?

Report to the class.

Istvan eats a lot of fruit.
Krisztina drinks three cups of coffee a day.
Zoltan doesn't eat a lot of meat.

(not) a lot of ▶ 25
Istvan eats **a lot of** fruit.
Zoltan does**n't** eat **a lot of** meat.

39

SKILLS: READING AND LISTENING

Pre-reading

1 Put these words into four groups.

Meat   Fruit   Vegetables   Milk products

cheese	beef
chicken	chips
pineapple	banana
onion	tomato
bacon	milkshake
icecream	strawberry
apple	lettuce
cucumber	

2 Can you add more words to each list?

Reading

3 Read the descriptions below and match the description with the picture.

THE BEST BURGER IN TOWN

Where's the best burger in the city? We went to five burger bars and this is what we found.

A BetterBurgers *(23 Marine Parade, 867 4639)*
The basic Beefburger ($6) is good value. It has 250g of good beef, lettuce and onions, and it comes with a lot of chips and cucumber salad. The banana milkshake ($3) is extra.

B The Real McCoy *(576 First Avenue, 454 0389)*
The service is slow but the burgers are good. Best is the Gorgonzola Burger: real Gorgonzola cheese, bacon, onions and 200g of tasty beef. Good value at $10. This comes with a lettuce salad (small). A Coke costs $2.

C The Fifties Cafe *(50 Eleventh Avenue, 475 8473)*
Try the ChickenBurger: grilled chicken with onions, and a side salad of tomato and lettuce, all for $5. Chips are extra ($2). The strawberry milkshakes ($4) are good: they use real strawberries.

D Heavens Above *(378 Bridge Street, 387 1000)*
Their vegetarian burgers are famous. We had a Hawaii Burger: pineapple with cheese and lettuce ($5); this comes with apple and cucumber salad, chips, and strawberry icecream. Good value.

E The Dakota *(227 Marine Parade, 867 3098)*
The Gorilla Burger – 300g of beef, chicken and bacon – is enormous, but expensive ($12). It comes with a lettuce salad and chips. The milkshakes are expensive, too ($6).

1

2

3

Comprehension check

4 Answer these questions.

  a Where does the burger cost $10?

  b Where does the milkshake cost $6?

  c How much beef is there in a Gorilla Burger?

  d How much beef is there in a Gorgonzola Burger?

  e What's in a Hawaii Burger?

  f How much is a chickenburger and a milkshake at the Fifties Cafe?

  g How much is a Hawaii Burger, chips, salad and ice cream?

Pre-listening

5 Match the picture with the word.

  packet   bottle   carton   can

Listening

6 📼 Listen and make a shopping list.

Speaking

7 Dictate a shopping list to your neighbour.

Adjectives

1 Match the opposites.

old	long
big	white
short	bad
hot	small
cheap	new
black	cold
good	expensive

This/that; these/those ▶ 26

2 Write dialogues.

(book – big?)
A: *Can you pass me that book?*
B: *This big book?*
A: *No, that small book.*

a (folder – black?)
b (pencil – long?)
c (coffee – black?)
d (newspapers – new?)
e (plates – hot?)
f (glasses – expensive?)

Food

3 Put the food into two groups:

COUNTABLE	UNCOUNTABLE
olives	*olive oil*

cheese	ice cream	ice
eggs	tomatoes	beef
ham	sugar	chips
onions	coffee	
bananas	milk	

4 Add 5 more words to each list.

A/some ▶ 23

5 Complete with *a/an* or *some*.

a Would you like _____ milk in your coffee?
b Would you like _____ banana milkshake?
c Would you like _____ ham in your pizza?
d Would you like _____ onions in your hamburger?
e Would you like _____ drink with your pizza?
f Would you like _____ salt on your chips?
g Would you like _____ cup of coffee?
h Would you like _____ ice in your drink?

How much/how many ▶ 27

6 Complete the sentences with *how much* or *how many*.

a _____ eggs do we have?
b _____ ice cream would you like?
c _____ beef is there in a Beefburger?
d _____ milk would you like?
e _____ sugar do you take?
f _____ coffee have we got?
g _____ onions would you like?
h _____ ham is there in a hamburger?

7 Complete the dialogue.

I'm going to the market.
a Can you get _____ olive oil?
b How _____ ?
c One bottle. And can you get _____ olives?
d How _____ ?
e 200g. And can you get _____ onions?
f How _____ ?
g A kilo. And _____ milk?
h _____ ?
i A carton. And _____ beef?
j _____ ?
Half a kilo.
k And can you get _____ packet of coffee?
OK.

8 Write dialogues for these situations:

9 What is happening?

Use these verbs:

cook   swim   drink   eat
talk   read

Bruce is swimming.

10 Make excuses:

Bruce, can you answer the phone?
No, I'm swimming.

1 Sheila …
2 Wayne …
3 Barry …
4 Kylie …
5 Stavros …

43

Pre-listening

1 What's in a pizza? Make a list.

cheese
tomatoes
olives

Listening

2 🔊 Listen to the conversation.
What does she order?
Complete the form.

3 Listen again.
What's in the Pizza Margarita?
What's in the Pizza Roma?
What's in the Pizza Primavera?
What's in the Pizza Veneciana?
What's in the Pizza Hawaii?

4 Listen again and write the address and telephone number.

FAST PIZZA

ORDER FORM

Pizza	Number	Size		
		s	m	b
Margarita				
Veneciana				
Hawaii				
Roma				
Primavera				
Drinks				
Coca cola				
Seven-up				
Diet coke				

Address:

Telephone:

5 Listen and complete these sentences.

A: Hello. Fast Pizza. Can _____ ?
B: Yes, _____ two pizzas, _____ .
A: Certainly. What kind _____ ?
B: _____ vegetarian pizzas?
A: Yes. _____ a plain Pizza Margarita.
B: _____ that?
A: Cheese and tomato. With garlic _____ .
B: _____ ?

Pre-writing

6 Read these letters.

Monday 12th

Dear Elvira,
It's Ivan's birthday on Saturday. Would you like to come
to dinner? Birget and Wally will be there. Can you bring
some music?

Hope you can come.

Lucia.

Wednesday 14th

Dear Lucia,
I'd love to come. Can I stay the night? I'll bring the new
Aerosmith CD.

See you Saturday,

Elvira.

Writing

7 Write a letter, inviting another student to lunch, or to a party, or to stay the weekend.

8 Read another student's letter and write a reply.

Speaking

9 Invite other students to a party. How many students can you invite?
If you can't go to the party, make an excuse.

I'm sorry, I'm going to Mona's party.

45

STUDY FOCUS

Check your grammar

This/that; these/those

1 Complete with *this*, *that*, *these*, or *those*.

How much is _____ pineapple?

How much is _____ pineapple?

How much are _____ watermelons?

How much are _____ watermelons?

Countables and uncountables

2 True or false?

   a Use *how much* for countable nouns.
   b Use *a/an* for singular countable nouns.
   c Use *some* for singular uncountable nouns.
   d Use *how many* for uncountable nouns.

Present continuous

3 Complete this table.

I *am* writing.
She _____ swimming
They _____ working.
Stavros and Sheila _____ cooking.
Barry _____ drinking.
What _____ you doing?
What _____ Wayne doing?

Build your Vocabulary

Quantities

Answer these questions.

   a How many metres are there in a kilometre?
   b How many centimetres are there in a metre?
   c How many millimetres are there in a centimetre?

Make questions and answers:

   d grams/kilogram?
   e kilograms/tonne?
   f centilitres/litre?

Practise your pronunciation

/ ð / / s / / z /

1 Practise saying these sentences.

   a How much is this pizza?
   b How much are these scissors?
   c How much are those crisps?
   d How much is that box of matches?
   e How much is the chicken and chips?
   f How much is this Swiss cheese?
   g How much are six of these sweets?

Linking

2 🔊 Listen. How many words can you hear?
Now repeat the sentences.

Unit 6 Things I like

1 What are the activities?

playing tennis	skiing	riding a motorbike
riding a horse	driving	playing basketball
playing the guitar	playing the piano	singing

1
2
3
4
5
6
7
8
9

2 Put the activities into three groups.

3 What are their names? Listen to the teacher.
Write the names under the pictures.

▶ Present simple – likes
▶ *Can* (ability)
▶ Possessive adjectives
▶ Apostrophe *'s*
▶ *Well* (adverb)

1 Can you do these things?

Ask each other: *Can you do that?*

> **Ability**
> *Can* ▶ **12**
> I **can** read Italian but I
> **can't** write it.

2 Can you speak any of these languages? How well can you speak
them? Can you read or write in any of these languages?

French   Portuguese   GREEK   Chinese
Spanish   Arabic   Italian
RUSSIAN   English   Turkish   German

Ask other students:

Can you speak …?
I can read it quite well but I can't write it very well.

> **Well** ▶ **19**
> I can read French quite
> **well**.
> I can't write it very **well**.

3 Look at the pictures.
Whose guitar is it? *Libby's.*
Whose skis are they?

Ask your neighbour
questions.

4 Make sentences about Libby,
Guy and Jethro.

Libby likes playing tennis.
She can type.

Who can paint?
Who can type?
Who likes Beethoven?
Who can play the guitar?
What does Guy like doing?
What sort of music does
   Jethro like?
What does Libby like
   playing?
What sports does Jethro like?

Libby

Guy

Jethro

5 What are Guy's questions?

6 Ask each other the questions in Activity 5.
Tell the class.

Paola likes pop music. Giovanni likes basketball …

7 Write a questionnaire. Send it to another student.

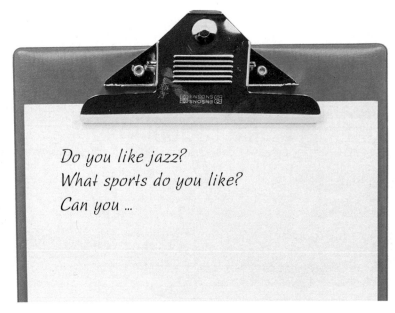

Do you like jazz?
What sports do you like?
Can you …

8 You are a street performer.
You want a partner. Choose
one thing you can do in each
list. Ask other students. Can
you find a partner?

dance
the tango
the cancan
rock and roll

sing
opera
the blues
rap

play
the guitar
the violin
the drums

SKILLS: READING AND LISTENING

Pre-reading

1 Make two lists:

Things I like   **Things I don't like**

Compare with another student.

Reading

2 Read this interview with film director Pedro Almodóvar.
Put the photos below into two groups:

Things Almodóvar likes.   **Things he hates.**

1   **2**   **3**   **4**   **5**   **6**

   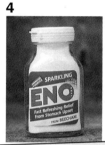  

Things I like
Reading in bed or on planes
Beginning each day, going down to my favourite café,
  reading the papers and having breakfast.
Playing table tennis.
Caribbean culture.
Traditional Spanish cooking.
The idea of coming back to Madrid after a long
journey.
'Eno' lemon fruit salts, with Vitamin C.

Things I don't like
The idea that someone is writing my biography.
Track suits.
Watching TV.
Any noise early in the morning.
Racism.
People who call themselves intellectuals.
Life in the big cities.
Life in the country.
Questionnaires of the type: 'Things I like, things I
  don't like'.

Listening

3 📼 Listen to this conversation and complete the forms.
What do they both like doing?

<table>
<tr><td colspan="2">**MATCHMAKERS**</td><td>1</td></tr>
<tr><td colspan="2">COMPUTER DATING</td><td></td></tr>
<tr><td>Name:</td><td></td><td></td></tr>
<tr><td>Age:</td><td></td><td></td></tr>
<tr><td>Interests:</td><td></td><td></td></tr>
<tr><td>Sports:</td><td></td><td></td></tr>
</table>

<table>
<tr><td colspan="2">**MATCHMAKERS**</td><td>2</td></tr>
<tr><td colspan="2">COMPUTER DATING</td><td></td></tr>
<tr><td>Name:</td><td></td><td></td></tr>
<tr><td>Age:</td><td></td><td></td></tr>
<tr><td>Interests:</td><td></td><td></td></tr>
<tr><td>Sports:</td><td></td><td></td></tr>
</table>

4 Listen to the second interview again, and write the questions.

5 Role play

Student A
You are looking for a partner. Complete this form. Use your imagination! Answer Student B's questions.

MATCHMAKERS
COMPUTER DATING
Name:
Age:
Interests:
Sports:

Student B
You work in a dating agency. Ask Student A questions and complete this form.

MATCHMAKERS
COMPUTER DATING
Name:
Age:
Interests:
Sports:

GRAMMAR AND VOCABULARY

Sports/activities

1 What are the activities?

2 Write questions.
I like football. (play / watch)
Do you like playing football or watching football?

a I like guitar music.
(play / listen to)
b I like poetry.
(read / write)
c I like food.
(cook / eat)
d I like tennis.
(play / watch)
e I like photos.
(take / look at)
f I like English.
(speak / read)

Possession ▶ 29

3 Make questions and answers.

guitar – Libby
Whose guitar is it? It's Libby's.

a computer – Jethro
b skis – Jethro
c piano – my brother
d bicycle – my best friend
e drums – Guy
f tennis racket – Libby
g books – the teacher
h car – the neighbour

4 Add apostrophes.

a What are your names?
b My names Adrian.
My brothers names Alexis.
c Is this your bag?
No, its my brothers.
d Whose are these cigarettes?
Theyre my brothers.
I dont smoke. Thats his bag.

Ability – *can* ▶ 12

5 Make true sentences using this table.

My best friend	can't	swim.
My brother	can	speak English.
My sister		cook.
		play the guitar.
		paint.
		ski.
		sing.
		read Chinese.
		drive.

Well ▶ 19

6 Add *well, quite well* or *very well* to the sentences in Exercise 3.

7 Write six sentences about famous people, using *well*.

Romario can play football very well.

Like ▶ 18

8 Complete these sentences with *like* or *likes*.

    a Margot _____ classical music and jazz.
    b Kenny doesn't _____ classical music but he _____ jazz.
    c What kind of music do you _____?
    d What kind of music does Adrian _____?
    e James and Rita both _____ football.
    f Eva _____ basketball but she doesn't _____ football.
    g Do you _____ Nirvana?
    h Does your friend _____ Spanish music?

9 Choose the correct form of the verb.

    a Can you (sing/singing)?
    b Do you like (play/playing) tennis?
    c Paola doesn't like (watch/watching) TV.
    d Manoli can (speak/speaking) English very well.
    e Fernando likes (drive/driving).
    f Emilio can't (drive/driving).

10 Make these sentences negative.

    a I can speak Japanese.
    b Alain likes Indian food.
    c My sister is married.
    d We like watching TV.
    e Lourdes can ski.
    f Katerina lives with her parents.
    g I'm English.
    h I speak English.
    i I can speak English.
    j I like English.

11 Complete the dialogue with these words.

well   music   languages
ski   sports   speak
favourite   play

    a What sort of _____ do you like?
        I like rock music.
    b What's your _____ group?
        Genesis.
    c Can you _____ the guitar?
        No, I can't.
    d What _____ do you play?
        I like swimming and tennis.
    e Can you _____?
    f Not very _____.
    g What _____ can you speak?
    h I can _____ Dutch and German.

Pre-writing

1 In groups of four, make true sentences.

One person likes …
Two people like …
Three people like …
We all like …
Nobody likes …

2 Do the same with *can*.

Pre-listening

3 Read this advertisement.

Are you aged 18 – 26?

Can you play a musical instrument?

Can you speak one European language?

Can you swim, play tennis, or ride?

And do you like working with children?

Would you like to work as a **CAMP COUNSELLOR** in an attractive European location this summer?

Write to:
CLP CAMPS
Box 8916
Brussels, Belgium

Listening

4 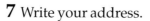 Listen to this interview. Put the information in order.

Sports
Nationality
Languages
Name   *1*
Other interests
Age
Musical instruments

5 Now complete the information.

Sports   *handball,*
Nationality
Languages
Name
Other interests
Age
Musical instruments

Writing

6 Imagine you want the job. Write a letter about yourself.

The Manager,
CLP CAMPS
Box 8916
Brussels, Belgium

Dear Sir/Madam,
I am interested in a job as Camp Counsellor. My name is …… and I come from …… I like ……

Yours faithfully,

7 Write your address.

6

Check your grammar

Can

1 Make the negative and question.

She can ski.
You can speak English very well.

Like

2 Complete this table.

I *like* playing tennis.
She _____ playing tennis.
We _____ playing tennis.
They _____ playing tennis.

Do you like playing tennis?
_____ she like playing tennis?
_____ they like playing tennis?

I *don't* like playing tennis.
He _____ like playing tennis.
We _____ like playing tennis.
They _____ like playing tennis.

Build your Vocabulary

Types of music

1 Make a list of different types of music.

rock
opera

Languages

2 What languages do they speak in
_____?

Country	Language
Holland	*Dutch*
France	
Greece	
Egypt	
Brazil	
Denmark	
Japan	
Chile	
Canada	
Switzerland	

Practise your pronunciation

Can/can't

1 ▭ What do you hear?
Can or *can't*?

2 /kæn/ or /kən/?
Listen to the cassette. Mark each example of *can* with either S (strong) or W (weak).

A I can dance the lambada. Can you dance the lambada?
B Yes, I can. I can dance it and I can play it on the piano.
A Can you?

Now, repeat the conversation.

Unit 7 I'm going to fly

1 Would you like to go to …?
Ask other students:

Would you like to go to …? Why? (Why not?)

2 Report. Tell the class about other students.

Tibor would like to go to Egypt. He likes Egyptian Art.

▶ *Was/were*
▶ Past simple
▶ *Going to*: intentions

1 Read the dialogue and complete the chart.

A: Where were you yesterday?
B: What was yesterday?
A: It was Tuesday.
B: I was in the library. Ask Ruth and Janet. We were all in the library. And Derek, too.
A: Ruth and Janet were in class. And Derek was at home.
B: Oh.

I *was*
we _____
you _____
he/she _____
they _____
it _____

Practise the dialogue.

Was/were ▶ 2
Where **were** you yesterday?
Derek **was** at home.
---

2 Ask each other:

Where were you yesterday?
at ten o'clock?
on Sunday evening?

3 Can you solve the problem? What did they do last summer? Read the sentences and complete the chart.

One person went to Turkey and stayed with friends.
One person went to India and went by plane.
Robin didn't go to Scotland.
Jon stayed in a youth hostel.
Anna didn't stay with friends.
Robin went by bus.
One person went to Scotland by bike.
One person went by plane and stayed in a hotel.

	Robin	Anna	Jon
country			
accommodation			
transport			

Past simple ▶ 7
Robin **went** by bus.
Jon **stayed** in a youth hostel.
Robin **didn't go** to Scotland.
---

4 Complete this conversation:

Travel agent: Can I help you?
You: Yes, I'd like an interesting holiday.
Travel agent: Something different?
You: Yes. Different from last year.
Travel agent: Where did you go last year?
You: I went …
Travel agent: How did you go?
You: I went …
Travel agent: Where did you stay?
You: I stayed …
Travel agent: …?
You: …

5 Ask each other about the last holiday. Report to the class.

Angela went to Switzerland. She stayed with friends …

6 Four friends are planning a holiday in France. How are they going to travel?

> **Going to ▶ 11**
> What **is** she **going to** do?
> She**'s going to** study.

7 What are they going to do in France?

He's going to study French.

8 What are the questions?

1 *I'm going to France.*
2 *I'm going to take the ferry.*
3 *I'm going to pick grapes.*
4 *In a French farmhouse.*
5 *For a month.*

STUDY FRENCH IN FRANCE!
Short intensive courses.
Stay with French families.

INTERLANGUE
Tel: 010 33 1 45 66 8429

Houseboat holidays

Explore the canals of France
Stay on a traditional houseboat

Write:
Houseboat Holidays

Working holidays in France
- Pick grapes in the Loire valley.
- Stay in a French farmhouse.

Tel:

SEE FRANCE BY BIKE
Mountain bike tours of France.

Bed and breakfast accommodation.
For more information, write to:

Pre-reading

1 How many different kinds of holidays can you think of?

skiing holiday
camping holiday

Reading

2 Read these holiday advertisements. How many activities can you find?

1 SET SAIL AND DISCOVER

...HURGHADA, one of Egypt's foremost resorts for every kind of water sport imaginable from sailing and windsurfing to scuba diving and deep sea fishing.

2 Plus travel

Fantastic Skiing!
Fantastic prices!

Switzerland: Saas Fee; Hotel Artemis from £395 per week inc. flight, transfers and halfboard.

071 259 0199

3 Britain's Best Boating

From England and Wales to Scotland, your best choice of boating holidays on all Britain's waterways and canals. From £70 per person per week. For your brochure write to Hoseasons holidays, Lowestoft, NR32 2LW today or ring 0502 501 501.

HOSEASONS

4 ADVENTURE HOLIDAYS IN SCOTLAND AND WALES

All year round
Rafting, Canoeing and Rock Climbing
from £225 per week, all included
Call 0678 76589

5 CYCLING or WALKING

IN BEAUTIFUL FRANCE
Relaxing summer holidays in beautiful out-of-the-way settings.
From £99 per week.
Call now for our FREE colour brochure.

THE BEATEN TRACK
(0495) 652975

6 SWIMMING WITH DOLPHINS in the Bahamas

A unique opportunity to swim with one of the most beautiful members of the dolphin family – spotted dolphins

DISCOVER *the* **WORLD!**
Under the guidance of a dolphin expert, daily activities include swimming and snorkelling with the dolphins, studying and photographing their behaviour, and exploring their underwater environment. Travel and accommodation is aboard a 70 ft steel-hulled schooner. Meals are prepared by the ship's own cook and are delicious!

8 nights from **£1612**
Departures: May to August

For more information call
DISCOVER *the* **WORLD** on 06977 48356.
Operated exclusively with WHALE AND DOLPHIN CONSERVATION SOCIETY

3 Complete the chart.

	Country	Time	Activities	Total Price
1		*all year*		–
2			*skiing*	
3				
4				
5				
6				

4 Choose a holiday. Tell other students about it.

I'd like to go to ... because ...

Pre-listening

5 How do you pronounce these names?

Dublin
Belfast
Cork
Galway
Limerick
Waterford
Donegal

Listening

6 🖳 Listen to the first part of the conversation and draw a line on the map to show the man's journey.

Listen to the second part and draw the woman's journey.

7 Which journey was in the past and which journey is in the future?

8 Listen again and answer these questions.

  a How is he going to get to Dublin?
  b How long is he going to stay in Galway?
  c Where is he going to stay in Cork?
  d How did she go from Dublin to Donegal?

9 Make questions for these answers.

  a By train.
  b With her sister.
  c A few days.
  d By plane.

Speaking

10 Imagine a journey you are going to make. Where are you going to go? How are you going to travel? What are you going to do in each place? Tell your neighbour. Listen to your neighbour and draw a line to show the journey.

61

GRAMMAR AND VOCABULARY

Holiday activities

1 Name the different activities.

a

b

c

d

e

f

Dates and times

2 Complete, using *at*, *in*, *on*, or no preposition.

What are you going to do *at* the weekend?

1 Where were you ___ Saturday?
2 What are you going to do ___ the summer?
3 I was in the library ___ this morning.
4 I went to Scotland ___ August.
5 Bela went to England ___ 1993.
6 We are going to work ___ the weekend.
7 What are you going to do ___ summer?
8 Did you stay home ___ Monday?
9 Mario's going to New York ___ next year.

Was/were ▶ 2

3 Complete the dialogues, using *was* or *were*.

A: _____ you at work yesterday?
B: No, I _____ at home.
A: Why? _____ you ill?
B: No, it _____ Monday. I don't work on Mondays.

C: Where _____ Pat this morning?
D: She _____ at the hosptial.
C: Why? _____ she ill?
D: No, she works at the hospital.

E: I _____ late for my French class.
F: Why?
E: The bus _____ late. The teacher _____ angry. But the other students _____ late, too.

Past simple ▶ 7

4 Put the verbs in the past and complete the text.

stay   rent   buy   go
fly   drive   visit

Last summer we (1) _____ to Florida. We (2) _____ from London to Miami and then we (3) _____ a car and (4) _____ to Orlando. We (5) _____ in a 4-star hotel. We (6) _____ Disney World and Barry (7) _____ a cowboy hat.

5 Make questions for the text in Activity 4.

(1) *Where did they go last summer?*

6 Write about a journey you made. Where did you go? How? Where did you stay? What did you buy?

7 What *didn't* you do last weekend?

I didn't meet Tom Cruise.

Tell other students.

8 What are Marta's plans? Write sentences.

She's going to take the train to Edinburgh.

9 Write a conversation between Marta and a friend:

Friend: *What are you going to do in August?*
Marta: *I'm going to the Edinburgh Festival.*
Friend: *When …?*

Valid Off Peak as Advertised

No Photocard Required

Class	Ticket type	Price
S T D	Travelcard	£13.00X 15 AUG 95

Valid on

15 AUG 95   05585 3115W03

Number

Between

LONDON & EDINBURGH

Valid

ONE DAY

Hotel Rob Roy

**Wilkinson Walk
Brinklorn
Linthgow
EH4 6RP**

Dear Ms Martin,

We are pleased to confirm your reservation for a single room on the night of 15th – 18th August. We look forward to seeing you.

Valid Off Peak as Advertised

No Photocard Required

Class	Ticket type	Price
S T D	Travelcard	£13.00X 19 AUG 95

Valid on

19 AUG 95   08595 1815W73

Number

Between

EDINBURGH & LONDON

Valid

ONE DAY

One Day Travelcard

EDINBURGH FESTIVAL

APOLLO THEATRE
Edinburgh EH4 7NP
Box Office (0865) 244544

Othello

Vienna State Opera
16th August   EVENING
CIRCLE: B 31   7.30pm

CIRCLE: B 31
16th August
EVENING
7.30pm
£14.50

EDINBURGH FESTIVAL

GRAND THEATRE
Edinburgh EH4 7NP
Box Office (0865) 706 099

Yerma

National Theatre of Spain
18th August   EVENING
CIRCLE: A 24   8.00pm

£15.00 (inc VAT)

RETAIN THIS PORTION

CIRCLE: B 31
18th August
EVENING
8.00pm
£15.00

THIS PORTION TO BE GIVEN UP

EDINBURGH FESTIVAL

LITTLE THEATRE
Edinburgh EH4 6NQ
Box Office (0865) 225 430

Romeo and Juliet

Royal Ballet
17th August   EVENING
STALLS: F 17   7.45pm

£10.80 (inc VAT)

RETAIN THIS PORTION

THIS PORTION TO BE GIVEN UP

Pre-listening

1 Look at these people. What are they planning?

Listening

2 📼 Listen to these people talking about their work plans, and complete the chart.

	Last summer	This summer
1		
2		
3		
4		

Pre-writing

3 Tell the story of this holiday.

Writing

4 Use the pictures to write a postcard.

> Wednesday 12th May
> Alice Springs
>
> Dear ...
>
> We're having a wonderful time in Australia. We arrived in Sydney ...

7

STUDY FOCUS

Check your Grammar

Past simple: talking about the past

1 What is the past of these verbs? Which are regular and which are irregular?

go   stay   see   live
ride   work   rent   have
visit drive   buy   fly
take   walk

2 What are the questions?

Where _____?
    I was at home yesterday.
Where _____?
    I went to the zoo yesterday.
What _____?
    I studied French.
What _____?
    I had eggs for breakfast.

Which verbs take 'did' in the question: be, go, study, have?

Going to: plans

3 Complete:

I *am* going to work this
    summer.
You _____ going to work this
    summer.
She _____ going to work this
    summer.
We _____ going to work this
    summer.
They _____ going to work this
    summer.

Now, make these sentences negative:

*I'm not going to work this
summer.*

Build your Vocabulary

Activities with *go*

a   b   c

1 Check the meaning of these verbs, and complete the list.

to go shopping
to go cycling
to go swimming
to go sightseeing
to go climbing
to go _____ ing
to go _____ ing
to go _____ ing

Word field: Places to stay

2 Where do you stay when you are on holiday? Add words to
   this list.

at a hotel
with friends

Practise your pronunciation

Schwa /ə/

1 📼 Listen to the cassette and mark examples of /ə/.

A: Where were you yesterday?
B: What was yesterday?
A: It was Saturday.
B: I was at the cinema. With Derek and Janet.
A: Derek was here and Janet was at home.
B: Oh.

2 Now, practise the dialogue.

Unit 8 A nice place to live

1 Look at these different places to live.

Where is it? Who lives in it? Is it a nice place to live, do you think? Why/why not?

2 Where would you like to live? Why?

3 Choose one of these places and 'sell' it to other students.

LANGUAGE ACTIVITIES

▶ *Have got*
▶ *Had*
▶ *There is/are; was/were*
▶ *No*
▶ Comparatives
▶ *What/like* (description)

1 Describe one of these flats. Which one is it?

It's got two bedrooms.
There's a small garden.
There's no garage.
The bathroom is next to the kitchen.

a

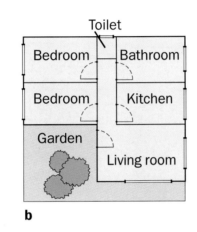

b

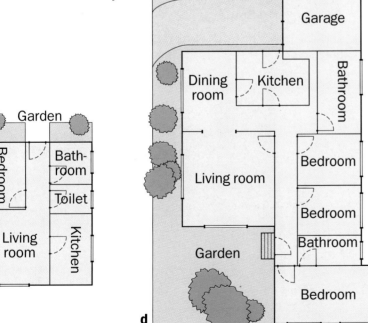

c

d

Description
Have got ▶ **10**
There is/are ▶ **17**
It**'s got** two bedrooms.
There**'s** a small garden.

No ▶ **22**
There's **no** garage.

2 Name the furniture and put it in the right room.

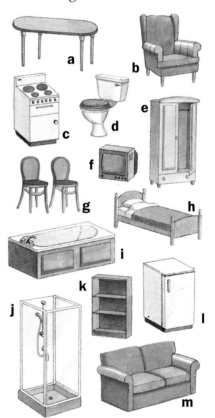

3 Draw a room and listen to the teacher.

Describe a room. Listen and draw.

There's a sofa on the left.
Next to the sofa there's a bookcase.

67

4 What are the questions?

I'm phoning about the flat ...
1 ...?
2 ...?
3 ...?
4 ...?
5 ...?

1 *It's in the centre of town.*
2 *It's got three bedrooms.*
3 *The living room is big and sunny.*
4 *No, there's no phone.*
5 *It's £350 a month.*

> **Description**
> **What's it like?** ▶ **18**
> **What's** the kitchen **like**?

5 Design a flat. Draw it. Is it furnished or unfurnished? Answer questions about it.

How many bedrooms has it got?
Are there any beds?
There are no chairs.

6 Look at the houses on the right. What's the difference? Which house is nicer?

This house is nicer than that house.
This house is more expensive.

> **Comparatives** ▶ **33**
> This house is nic**er than** that house.
> This house is **more expensive**.

Role play

7 Student A: Try and sell House A to Student B.
Student B: Try and sell House B to Student C.
Student C: Which house do you prefer?

8 Describe your own house or flat to other students.

9 Have you lived or stayed in another house or flat? What was it like?

There was a garden.
It had two bedrooms.
It was smaller/bigger than my flat now.

> **Description (past)**
> **There was/were** ▶ **17**
> **It had** ▶ **10**
> There **was** a garden.
> It **had** two bedrooms.

FOR SALE
£120,000
A

FOR SALE
£150,000
B

SKILLS: READING AND LISTENING

Pre-reading

1 Where would you find

a cottage?
a farmhouse?
a town house?
a beach house?
a block of flats?
a housing estate?

Reading

2 Read these advertisments and match the description with the picture.

a

SAAS FEE, SWITZERLAND.
Large one-bedroomed chalet overlooking lake in valley, 10 km from nearest town. Ideal for skiing holidays or long-let. Large open-plan kitchen/dining area with full central heating and double glazing. 1.3 m S.Francs

Telephone: 010 44 76530966

b

LARGE COTTAGE
with thatch in rural Devon, 5 km from Honiton. Surrounded by gardens with views of woodland. Three bedrooms, reception room, kitchen/breakfast room, living room with fireplace.

About £200,000

c

Barnes, London:
Large detached town house in convenient location. Mature gardens front and back, four bedrooms, living room, dining room, kitchen and conservatory at rear.

£198,000

d

DIDBURY, MANCHESTER. Compact terraced family house. Small garden at rear, with garden shed. 2 bedrooms, bathroom, reception room/kitchen and living/dining room. Patio doors leading to garden. Ideal for first time buyer.

Around £75,000

1

2

3

4

3 Write an advertisement for your dream home. Draw a picture, too!

Listening

4 🔊 Listen to this conversation and complete the information.

Address: _____
_____
_____
_____

Number of rooms: _____
Furnished/unfurnished:
_____

Rent: _____

5 Listen again and write the questions.

a _____ dining room?
b _____ kitchen _____?
c _____ separate toilet?
d _____ sunny?
e _____ furnished?
f How much _____?

Role Play

6 Student A: You have a flat to rent. What's it like? Answer Student B's questions.

Student B: You want to rent a flat. Phone Student A and ask about the flat.

69

Rooms

1 What is the name of the room or place?

a you sleep there   *bedroom*
b you eat there
c you cook there
d you wash there
e you keep your car there
f you sit and watch TV there
g you grow flowers there

Furniture

2 Write definitions of the following.

a bed   *You sleep in it*
b chair
c table
d fridge
e wardrobe
f bookcase
g bath
h cooker

Adjectives ▶ 31

3 Make one sentence.

There's a kitchen. It's small and modern.
There's a small modern kitchen.

a There's a garden. It's big and sunny.
b There are two beds. They are small and uncomfortable.
c There's a bathroom. It's small and modern.
d There's a sofa. It's big and _____.
e There's a garage. It's _____ and _____.
f There are four armchairs. They are _____ and _____.
g There's a bath. It's _____ and _____.
h There are three bedrooms. They are _____ and _____.

Description ▶ 17

4 Complete with *it* or *there*.

My flat is quite nice. _____'s got two big sunny bedrooms. _____'s a small living room. Next to the living room _____'s a kitchen. The kitchen is small and modern. _____'s got a fridge and a cooker. The bathroom is quite small. _____'s between the two bedrooms. _____'s got a bath and a shower. _____'s a separate toilet.

What…like? ▶ 18

5 Complete this dialogue.

A: Hello. I'm calling about the flat.
B: Yes?
A: _____ ?
B: It's very nice. It's got three bedrooms.
A: _____ ?
B: They are nice. One of them is a bit small but the other two are quite big.
A: _____ ?
B: It's small but modern. It's got a microwave and a fridge.
A: _____ ?
B: It's very nice. There's a big old bath and a toilet.
A: _____ ?
B: The living room is a bit small but it's very sunny. There are two balconies.
A: _____ ?
B: Well, they are typical balconies, really. Nothing special.

6 Describe an unfurnished flat.

There are no chairs.
There's no phone.

Comparatives ▶ 33

7 Make comparisons. Use these adjectives.

big	small
expensive	cheap
comfortable	uncomfortable
convenient	inconvenient
fast	slow

castle / house
A castle is bigger than a house.

a flat / palace
b tent / house
c caravan / tent
d skyscraper / castle
e houseboat / yacht

Description (past) ▶ 2,10

8 Complete this conversation.

A: I lived in the country when I was a child.
B: What was your house like?
A: It ____ big and old. It ____ five bedrooms and a big living room.
The kitchen ____ big too. But there ____ no cooker. There ____ a fireplace. There ____ no fridge, of course.
A: What ____ the bathroom like?
B: It ____ big and cold. It ____ a big old bath.
B: ____ there a garden?
A: Yes, there ____ a big garden, and there ____ fruit trees.

9 Compare two places you know. For example:

Your school and another school.
Your classroom and another classroom in your school.
Your office and another office in your building.
Two sports centres in your town.
Two department stores in your town.
Two universities in your city.

SKILLS: LISTENING AND WRITING

Pre-listening

1 What questions do you ask when you are choosing a place to live?

Is it cheap or expensive?
Is it near the shops?
Is it …?

Listening

2 🔲 Listen and complete the chart.

	Old flat/house	New flat/house	Problem
1			
2			
3			

Language focus

3 Listen again, and complete this text.

We lived in the country before, in a village, and we had
_____ house, with a _____ garden and so on. But
then we moved to the city, and now we live in a flat. It's
_____, of course. But we are lucky because there's a garden
– _____, and _____ for the children to play. The flat
is _____ than the house in the village. And there's no
garage, _____ problem, because we have to park the car on
the street. And _____ to find a place.

Pre-writing

4 Put this description in order.

The first bedroom is quite big.

There's a small bathroom opposite the second bedroom.

When you come in the front door, there's a living room on the right.

Then there are two bedrooms.

Next to the living room is the kitchen.

The second bedroom is very small.

It's a big, sunny flat.

1 *My flat is on the fifth floor.*

Writing

5 Write a description of your flat or house for a friend who hasn't seen it.

Check your grammar
Description

1 Make questions and negative sentences.

a There's a garden.
Is there a garden?
There's no garden.
b There's a garage.
c There are chairs.
d It's got a telephone.
e It's got three bedrooms.

Comparatives

2 What's the rule?

Adjective	Comparative
small	smaller
sunny	sunnier
expensive	more expensive
comfortable	more comfortable

Complete:
old _____
nice _____
convenient _____
uncomfortable _____

Build your Vocabulary
Adjectives

1 What are the opposites?

expensive
big
tall
wide
fast
low
new
good
furnished
comfortable

Word field: furniture

2 Add words to these lists.

kitchen	living room	bathroom	bedroom
cooker	sofa	bath	bed
fridge			

Practise your pronunciation
Sentence stress

1 Mark the main stress in these sentences.

A: There's a bookcase on the left.
B: No, there's a bookcase on the right.

A: There's a bookcase on the left.
B: No, there's a television on the left.

A: There's a table in the bedroom.
B: No, there's a table in the kitchen.

A: There's a table in the bedroom.
B: No, there's a bed in the bedroom.

A: There's a toilet in the garden.
B: No, there's a toilet in the bathroom.

A: There are some chairs in the garage.
B: No, there's a sofa in the garage.

2 🔲 Listen and check.

3 Practise saying the sentences with another student.

Unit 9 It's just a game

STARTING POINTS

1 Can you find these things in the pictures?

jungle	monster
skyscraper	ship
dinosaur	helicopter
robot	snake

2 Describe one of these scenes to other students. Can they guess which scene it is?

a

b

c

d

LANGUAGE ACTIVITIES

▶ *Have to*
▶ *Should*

1 Read these descriptions and match the description with the picture in Starting Points.

1 Aztec Gold

You are an explorer in the Amazon jungle. You have to find the treasure of the Aztecs. On your way you meet snakes, alligators, and other horrors. When you get to the Aztec ruins, there is one last obstacle: the curse of Quetzocoatl! Action-packed! Don't miss it!

2 The Mountain of the Moon

Jason has to cross the sea and reach the Mountain of the Moon. On the way he meets monsters, loses his ship, and gets lost in the Labyrinth. You have to rescue him, find his ship, and lead him to the Mountain of the Moon. Great graphics but boring.

3 Last Exit

You have to escape from the city before nightfall. You get lost on the underground, helicopters chase you, you fight a motorbike gang. And it's getting late! Something for everyone. Highly recommended.

2 Read the descriptions again and complete the chart.

Game	Object	Obstacles	Recommendation
Aztec Gold			Don't miss it.
	rescue Jason		
		helicopters motorbike gang	

Have to ▶ 15
Jason **has to** cross the sea.
You **have to** escape.

75

3 Design a video game of your own, using these ideas. Explain it to other students.

Setting	Object	Obstacles
Ancient Egypt	*find pyramid*	
Outer space	*come home*	*robot*
Under the sea		
Jurassic period		

4 Tell the story of a favourite video game, or an adventure film that you like.

You should see this film. It's about a ... He/she has to ...
You should play this game. There's a ... He/she has to ...

5 What's your opinion?

Video games are good for children.
Video games shouldn't be violent.
Children should read books, not watch TV or play video games.
All children should learn to use computers.
All school classrooms should have computers.

Discuss in pairs or groups and report.

We think ...
We don't think ...

Should ▶ 14
You **should** see this film.

---

6 Think of things you have to do every day, and things you should do, but don't.

I have to go to work.
I should help my brother with his homework, but I don't.

Think of things you shouldn't do.

I shouldn't watch TV so much.

Make sentences about your friends and family too.

My father shouldn't work so much.

Pre-reading

COMPUTERS TURNED MY BOY INTO A ROBOT

I HAD TO TURN OFF ELECTRICITY SAYS MUM

1 Look at this headline and picture. What is the article about?

Reading

2 Read the article. How was Paul like a 'robot'?

A mother says that her schoolboy son's addiction to computers turned him into a 'robot'.

Paul, now 19, was a computer addict.

'He didn't want to eat or sleep' says Connie Bedworth, Paul's mother. 'He locked himself in his bedroom. He sat there all day – all night, too.'

'One night I had to turn off the electricity. It was the only way to make him stop.' Connie bought Paul his computer when he was 11. 'I thought it would help him in his school work'.

At first Paul played computer games. Then he started writing his own programmes. When he was 14 he learned how to enter secret computer systems. He discovered top secret information.

But yesterday a court in London decided Paul was not guilty of breaking the law. 'He's not a criminal: he's a computer addict', they said.

Not any more, says Paul. 'That part of my life is finished.' Paul is now a student at Edinburgh University.

adapted from article in Daily Mirror March 18 1993

Comprehension check

3 Are these statements true or false?

a Paul's mother bought him the computer.

b He was 14 when he started playing computer games.

c Paul went to court because he discovered secret information.

d He is a criminal.

e He is not a computer addict now.

Roleplay

4 Student A: You are a newspaper reporter. Ask Paul about his computer addiction.

Student B: You are Paul. Answer questions about your computer addiction.

When did you get your first computer?

Pre-listening

5 Who should you see if you've got a problem?

A problem with your health?   *You should see a doctor.*
A problem with your teeth?
A problem with your computer?
A problem with your animals?
A problem with your house/flat?
A problem with your money?
A problem with your English?

Listening

6 📼 Listen to this radio programme and fill in the chart.

	Problem	Solution
1		
2		
3		

7 What do you think of the solutions? Good or bad?

8 Listen again, and complete these sentences.

a _____ my son plays video games.
b _____ buy him some educational games.
c _____ my neighbours. They play heavy metal music day and night.
d _____ talk to them.
e _____ our cat chases dogs.
f _____ take it to the vet.

Speaking

9 Imagine a problem – with your pets, family, friends …
Tell other students. Who gives the best advice?

My problem is: My best friend …

Geography

1 Find these words in the picture.

mountain   river
island   forest
cave   sea
lake   city

Think of an example of a mountain, an island, etc.

Mount Kilimanjaro.
Easter Island.

Action verbs

2 Which of these verbs are regular in the past, and which are irregular?

get lost
lose
find
meet
escape
chase
get to
rescue

Write a story using five of these verbs. Put the verbs in the correct form.

Last summer I went for a walk in the mountains. It started to rain and I got lost …

There is/are ▶ 17

3 Complete the sentences, using *there, it* or *they*.

There is a castle on the mountain. *It* is big.

a _____ is a bridge over the river. _____ is old.
b _____ are two islands in the lake. _____ are small.
c _____ is a forest on the mountain and _____ is a cave in the forest. _____ is small and dark.
d In the cave _____ is some treasure. _____ are two monsters in front of the cave. _____ are hungry.

4 Write complete sentences.
Theseus in the Labyrinth

Theseus / find / Ariadne   *Theseus has to find Ariadne.*
First / he / kill / the monster.
Then / escape / the Labyrinth.
You / rescue / him.
Then / Theseus and Ariadne / reach / Naxos.
You / help / them.

5 Make a story.

Kentucky Smith	gets lost	in the Himalayas.
Princess Ada		in the Sahara desert.
		in the …

He	has to	get to	the …
She		reach	
		escape from	
		rescue	
		climb	

| He | meets | the … |
| She | loses | |

He	has to	find	the …
She		chase	
		fight	
		kill	

Have to ▶ 15

6 Complete, using the correct form of *have to*.

Would you like to watch TV?
No, I <u>have to</u> do my homework.

a Would you like to meet for lunch tomorrow?
   No. Tomorrow I _____ do the cleaning.
b Is Josef free this evening?
   No, Josef _____ cook dinner.
c Is Margarita free?
   No, Margarita _____ do the shopping.
d Nurses _____ work at night.
e My sister and I _____ study this weekend.
f Do you _____ study French?
   No. It's not compulsory.
g What time do you _____ go to bed?
   I _____ go to bed before midnight.

7 Write sentences about things these people have to do.

a The Queen.
   The Queen has to smile a lot.
b A policeman or
   policewoman.
c A football player.
d A comedian.
e A teacher.
f A doctor.
g A student of English.

Should ▶ 14

8 Give some advice to a friend who is

a a smoker
b addicted to computers
c fat
d always angry
e always sad
f addicted to work

9

SKILLS: LISTENING AND WRITING

Pre-listening

1 Match the picture with the verb.

go through   go over
go down   go across
go around   go up

Speaking

3 Draw a map, with mountains, rivers, lakes etc. Show it to your neighbour. Tell them where to find the treasure.

You have to go over the mountains, go down the river … and the treasure is …

Listening

2 📼 Look at the map and listen to the directions. Where is the treasure?

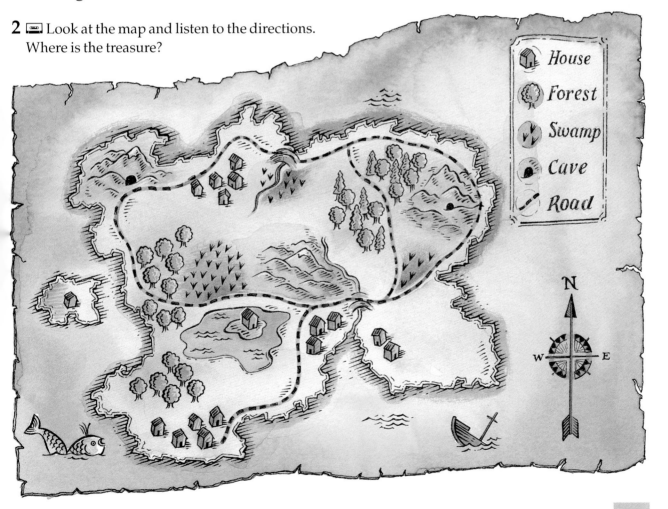

Writing

4 Have you seen these films?

a

b

c

d

Which film is this one?

It's about a young boy: his parents go away and leave him alone in the house. Two thieves try to get in the house and the boy has to fight them. It's a good film: you should see it.

Write about a film you have seen and that you liked.

It's about …

STUDY FOCUS

Check your grammar

Have to/should

1 *Should* or *have to*?

a You _____ wear a hat.
b You _____ stop.
c You _____ go back.
d You _____ read.
e You _____ see this play.
f You _____ drink milk.

2 Make questions.

Does he have to work?   Yes, he has to work.

a _____ ?   Yes, they have to speak English.
b _____ ?   Yes, she should phone.
c _____ ?   Yes, she has to stay home.
d _____ ?   Yes, he should see a doctor.

Build your Vocabulary

Prepositions of movement

1 Complete these sentences with the best preposition.

a Walk *over* the bridge.
b Go _____ the forest.
c Climb _____ one side of the mountain and _____ the other side.
d Walk _____ the tunnel.
e Run _____ the tree.
f Swim _____ the bridge.
g Drive _____ the lake.

Word family: journeys

2 Put these words into the boxes in the diagram.

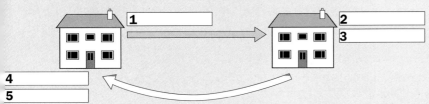

leave   return   come back
arrive   get to

Practise your pronunciation

1 Which words rhyme (have the same sound)?

a would   wood   cold
b good   old   should
c food   good   would
d gold   should   cold
e sword   word   bird
f blood   wood   good
g should   sold   would

2 🎧 Listen and check.

3 Practise saying the words.

Unit 10 It's the latest

1 This is a street in the 1880s.

This is the same street now. What has changed?

2 Talk about the place where you live. What was it like before? What's it like now?

LANGUAGE ACTIVITIES

▶ Present perfect
▶ Superlatives
▶ Directions
▶ Impersonal *you*

1 What's in fashion? What's out of fashion?

Make two lists, then compare with other students. Think of

	In	Out
Clothes, hair-styles		
short skirts		
long skirts		
Types of music		
Singers/goups/actors		
Places		
cafés		
bars		
clubs		
Technology		
cassettes		
virtual reality		
Food		
pizza		
ice cream		

2 Are you **In**?

Prepare a questionnaire to ask other students.
For example:

Have you seen the latest ... film/video?
Have you heard the latest ... single/CD?
Have you been to the new ... shop/disco/club?
Have you tried the new ... ice cream/perfume?

Ask for opinions, too:

What did you think of it?

> **Present perfect ▶ 9**
> **Have you been** to Dillons?
> No, I **haven't**.

3 What's the best ...? Ask other students.

What's the best bookshop in town?
Have you been to Dillons? That's quite good.

Report to the class.

Diego thinks Virgin is the best music store in town ...

> **Superlatives ▶ 34**
> What's **the best** bookshop?
> Have you heard **the latest** ...?

4 Where do you do these things in your country?

buy newspapers
buy stamps
eat fast food
change money
buy a map
buy aspirins
catch a taxi
buy bus tickets
have a coffee

Ask other students.

Where do you have a coffee in your country?

> **Impersonal 'you' ▶ 39**
> **You buy** stamps at a post office.

5 Where's the Post Office?
Give instructions.

*You go down this street. Then
you take the first street ...*

> **Directions ▶ 39**
> How do you get to the
> station?
> You go down this street.
> Then you cross the square.

6 Practise short conversations.

hotel?
Burger King?
museum?
etc

Excuse me?
Yes?
Is there a ... near here?
Yes, ...

7 How do you get to your home? Give instructions.

Take bus number ...
Take the train from ... to ...
Get out at ...

Ask about other places in the city or town where you are.

How do you get to the city centre from here?

Role play

8 In the tourist information
office.

Student A: Imagine you are a
tourist in the town you are in
now. Ask as many questions
as possible.

Student B: Answer Student
A's questions.

*I have to change money. Is there a
bank near here?*

*Yes, there's one on King William
Street.*

SKILLS: READING AND LISTENING

Pre-reading

1 Look at the pictures. What are they?

a

b

c

d

e

Reading

2 Read the fashion news and match the article with the picture.

1 **THEY'RE BACK AND THEY'RE HOT!**
Now that spring has arrived, it's time to put away your chunky winter sweaters, and welcome back the V-neck. V-necks are back in fashion, and not just with golfers and schoolchildren. *Everyone's* wearing them. Are you?

2 **JUST THE THING FOR GETTING ROUND TOWN AND COUNTRY:**
Combining an authentic American look with the latest in footwear technology, World Hikers are not only trendy – these boots are made for walkin'. Check 'em out!

3 **WATCH OUT FOR THE LATEST IN DESIGNER TRANSPORT:** These scooters are about to appear on a street near you!

Designed to look like Italian scooters of the Sixties, the Italuce is expected to be a big hit with fans of the 'retro' look.

4 **THE LATEST IN PEDAL POWER:** These laid-back bikes are the in-thing in California now: there are even specialist shops, clubs, and magazines for laid-back bikers. They're faster and more comfortable than your traditional bike, say the manufacturers. Just lie back and think of the £900 price tag.

5 **THE HOTTEST THING IN FOOTWEAR:**
The latest arrival from across the Atlantic, where it's very big, is the classic seventies basketball shoe re-styled for the nineties. They're 'Dr J's, and they're OK!

Word focus

3 Look at these dictionary definitions of words in the text. Find the definition that matches the meaning in the text.

> **hot** /hɒt/ *adj.* **1.** having a high degree of heat; **2.** has a burning taste; **3.** very recent, fashionable.
> **look** /lʊk/ *n.* **1.** an act of looking; **2.** appearance, style; **3.** expression of the face.
> **fan** /fæn/ *n.* **1.** something you use to make the air cool; **2.** a person who supports something, e.g. a sport, enthusiastically.
> **hit** /hɪt/ *n.* **1.** the act of hitting something; **2.** a popular success.
> **big** /bɪg/ *adj.* **1.** having a large size; **2.** very popular or successful.

Pre-listening

4 Why do you go to the places shown on the right?

You go to a post office to buy stamps.

Listening

5 🔊 Listen to these four short conversations. Where are they?

6 Listen again. In which conversation do you hear these expressions?

a I'll just have a look.
b I'm just looking, thanks.
c I'm just returning this.
d Can I try these on, please?
e What's the best rate?
f What size do you take?

Speaking

7 In pairs have shopping conversations in the following places.

post office
shoe shop
library

Shops

1 Write definitions.

shoeshop
You buy shoes at a shoeshop.

a bookshop
b newsagents
c pharmacy
d supermarket
e cinema
f restaurant
g coffee shop
h music shop
i post office

Two-part verbs

2 Complete with the correct verb.

get out
try on
take out
get on
get off

a When you ____ ____ the bus, cross the road and it's the first on the left.
b Excuse me, can I ____ these boots ____ ?
c Take a taxi and ____ ____ at Trafalgar Square.
d The train leaves in five minutes. You ____ ____ at Platform 6.
e I'd like to ____ this book ____ , please.

Present perfect ▶ 9

3 Make questions.

CD   *Have you heard the new Michael Nyman CD?*

a film
b book
c video game
d hair gel
e single
f video
g comic
h chocolate bar

4 Make eight true sentences using this table. Make sentences about yourself and about your friends.

I	have	seen	the new	[name]	CD
	haven't	been to	the latest		video
	has	heard			magazine
[Name]	hasn't	tried			film
		read			shop
		bought			programme

Vaclav hasn't seen the new David Byrne video.

Superlatives ▶ 34

5 Complete these short conversations.

A: It's a big shop.
B: *Big! It's the biggest!*

A: It's a new film.
B: _____

A: They're an old group.
B: _____

A: It's a cheap restaurant.
B: _____

A: It's a good programme.
B: _____

A: He's a great singer.
B: _____

6 Write directions using this map.

How do you get to the hotel?

Walk down this street, take the second street on the right, and it's on the left.

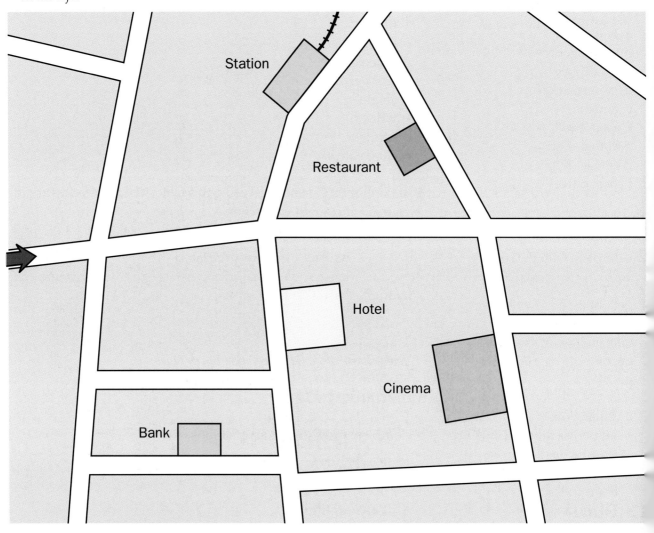

a How do you get to the bank?
b How do you get to the station?
c How do you get to the cinema?
d How do you get to the restaurant?

7 Draw a map of the streets around your school. Write directions for different places. Can other students follow the map?

Walk out of the school. Turn left …

8 Describe how you come to your school.

I take the bus to … I get out at … I walk down … street. I turn …

SKILLS: LISTENING AND WRITING

Pre-listening

1 Make sentences about this map using these expressions.

near   next to
opposite   between
in front of at the end of

The bus stop is in front of the entrance.

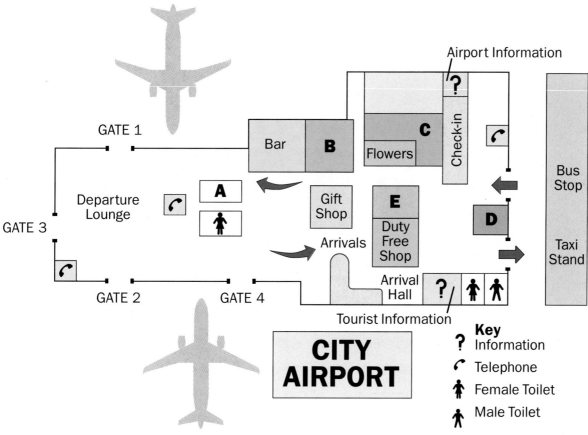

Listening

2 ▭ Listen to these conversations and identify the different places (A–E).

Writing

3 Write instructions to a friend, describing how to get to your home from the centre of the city, or from the station, or from the airport.

> *Dear ...,*
> *I'm looking forward to your visit. This is how to get to*
> *my place: First ...*

10

STUDY FOCUS

Check your grammar
Present perfect

1 What are the past participles of these verbs?

be
see
try
hear
buy
play
read

2 Make sentences, questions and negative sentences:

I've been there.   Have I been there?   I haven't been there.
You
She
They
Henri
We

Build your vocabulary
Word formation: compound nouns

1 What is one word for these definitions?

a shop for books = *a bookshop*

a a shop for shoes
b a place for parking cars
c a place where buses stop
d a shop for records
e a station for trains
f a building for offices

Word family: directions

2 What are the opposites?

over
back
inside
down
upstairs
behind

Practise your pronunciation
Key

1 ⌨ Listen to these questions. Are they high or low?

a Excuse me?
b Excuse me?
c Is there a bank near here?
d Where's the station?
e How do you get to the town centre?
f Can I help you?
g Can I try it on?
h Do you know how to use the phone?

What is the difference?
Which sounds more polite: high or low?

2 Practise asking the questions, politely.

1 Choose one of these people and describe him/her. Can other students guess who it is?

2 Can you guess their age, nationality and personality?

3 Describe another student in the class. Can other students guess who it is?

93

▶ *I (don't) think so.*
▶ *Look like*
▶ Present continuous (future use)

1 Why do people fall in love? What is important?

Put these in order of importance for you:

job
money
personality
looks
age
family
same interests
same outlook (opinions, beliefs)

other?

Compare with other students. Do you agree?

> **Agreeing/disagreeing ▶ 40**
> I agree. I think so, too.
> I don't agree. I don't think so.

2 Look at the people on page 91 again. There are eight people and they are all couples. Can you find the four couples? Report your decision. Do other students agree?

They (don't) look like a couple because …
I don't think so.

> **Look (+ like) ▶ 18**
> They **look like** a couple.
> Do you **look like** your sister?

3 One couple describe how they met. Which couple is it?

Gary Grabban: We met in the school playground in 1978. we were both fifteen. I went for her beauty, her smile, her outlook.

Yvonne Grabban: I loved his Finnish looks, blond hair and his big muscly legs (at the time he was a footballer). It was totally physical at first, but even then I thought: I'll marry him one day.

I think it is … because …

4 What do people talk about when they meet for the first time? For example, at a party?

the weather?
music?
food?
football?
school or work?
family?
politics?

Imagine a dialogue between two people. They are meeting for the first time. What is a good opening line?

Do you come here often?
Are you married?
Have we met before?
Are you a friend of …'s?
That's a nice shirt.
Nice weather we're having.
Would you like a drink?

Practise your conversation with another student. Perform it to the class.

Making arrangements
Present continuous ▶ 6
*What **are** you **doing** on Friday?*

5 The next day. What do they say on the telephone?

We met yesterday at …
Are you free on …?
What are you doing on …?
Would you like to go …?

Write the conversation, practise it, and perform it.

Speaking

6 Have a conversation with your neighbour about one of the topics in activity 4.

Pre-reading

1 Put these words into two groups.

friendly
handsome
caring
slim
attractive
loving
warm
well-built
sensitive

Physical	Personality

2 What are the opposites of the adjectives in activity one?

friendly   *unfriendly*

Reading

3 Read these 'lonely hearts' advertisements. Match each advertisement with a picture.

ATTRACTIVE, slim, 45-year-old businesswoman, enjoys tennis, cycling, hill walking, gardening. Seeks intelligent, caring partner (Non-smoker) with similar interests, age 40-50. Box 3478.

TALL, well-built male, 37, own flat, likes eating out, films, exhibitions; seeks similar female for lasting relationship. Box 9681.

HANDSOME professional male, 28, non-smoker, seeks friendly, slim, educated woman, same age, for dining out, theatre, countryside walks, friendship, maybe love. Box 6987.

GRADUATE woman, separated, thirty-something, looking to share good life with similar man. Interests: books, art, theatre, cinema, food and good conversation. Box 6008.

NEEDED: warm attractive woman by sensitive loving divorced man, 43, who enjoys music, sport and the outdoor life. Your telephone number, please. Box 4920.

INTELLIGENT, interesting professional woman, 26, slightly overweight, looking for an older, dependable man who likes eating out, long walks, and talking about the meaning of life.

4 Can you find some possible couples?

Listening

5  Listen to this conversation and put the topics in order.

    work/study
    computers
    music
    drinks
    common friends

6 Listen again, and complete the first part of the conversation.

A: Hello.
B: Hi.
A: _____ party?
B: Yes, thanks.
A: _____ Lisa's?
B: No, _____, _____ her brother's.
A: Oh. Ben?
B: Yeah. _____?
A: I'm _____. Actually, we
    _____ together.
B: Oh _____?
A: Yeah. My name's Errol, _____.
B: Hi. I'm Carol.
A: Karen?
B: Carol.
A: Oh. Carol. Hi. _____ a drink?
B: _____.

7 Listen again, and decide the meaning of these expressions.

    actually
    by the way
    oh
    I mean
    you know

Can you translate these expressions into your language?

Speaking

8 Practise saying the first part of the conversation in pairs.

Relationships

1 Match these expressions with their definition.

they are separated
they are divorced
he/she is widowed
they are engaged
he/she is single

two people have agreed to get married
a husband and wife agree to live separately
he/she is not married
his wife or her husband is dead
a husband and wife have ended their marriage

Nationalities: nouns and adjectives

2 Complete the chart.

Country	Person	Adjective
Finland	a Finn	Finnish
Italy	an Italian	
	a Pole	
		Spanish
Brazil		
Turkey		
	a Swede	
		German
Greece		
		Swiss
	a Portuguese	
	an Englishman/woman	
Australia		

Look + like ▶ 18

3 Complete the sentences with

look like
looks like

She *looks like* Princess Diana.

a He _____ Brad Pitt.
b Do you _____ your father?
c They both _____ their mother.
d Ellen _____ Kim Basinger.
e My brother doesn't _____ me.
f My sister _____ me.
g Who do you _____ ?

4 Who do *you* look like? Write four sentences.

I (don't) look like my …
My brother/sister looks like …

Agreeing/disagreeing ▶ 40

5 Make statements about other students and see if other students agree.

Kurt looks like Johnny Depp.
I agree/I don't agree.

Making arrangements ▶ 6

6 What has David arranged?

Monday: tennis – Jane
On Monday he's playing tennis with Jane.

a Tuesday: cinema – Alice
b Wednesday: lunch – Elvira
c Thursday: theatre – Harriet
d Friday: shopping – Janet
e Saturday: disco – Maggie
f Sunday: dinner – Francesca

SKILLS: LISTENING AND WRITING

Pre-listening

1 Find an example of

a concert
a film (or: a movie)
an exhibition
a sports event
a play

a

> **JUNIOR (PG)** Scwarzenegger gets pregnant in this Ivan Reitman comedy. *Clapham Picture House* : 1.30, 4.00, 6.30, 9.30; *Empire Leicester Square*: 1.00, 3.30, 6.00, 8.30, 11.00; *MGM Baker Street*: 1.20, 3.35, 6.00, 8.30.

b

> **ROYAL ACADEMY OF ARTS**
> Picadilly W1. 10-6 daily.
> Recorded info 071-439 4996/7
> The Painted Page: Italian Renaissance Book Illumination The Glory of Venice: 1700-1800 Closes Wednesday!

c

> **CYCLO-CROSS:**
> Oxonian CC Series (Oxford). The penultimate meeting in the five-event series returns to Oxford School, the venue for last year's veteran's championship. The main race is at 1.15 pm, following the under-12s event at 11.30 am and the juveniles race at noon.

d

> **QUEEN ELIZABETH HALL   Sunday 11 Dec 7.30**
> # GERMAN ROMANTIC
> *London Soloists Orchestra*
> Cello *F.M. Ormezowski*   Piano *Megumi Fujita*
> Violin *Arisa Fujita*   Conductor *Josefowitz*
>
> **SCHUMANN** *Piano Concerto*
> **BRAHMS** *Concerto for violin and cello*
> Beethoven *Romance*   Schubert *Concert Rondo*
> £7   £9   £12   £14   071 928 8800

e

> **UNICORN THEATRE**
> Gt. Newport St.
> London WC2
> *The only West End Theatre for children and their families*
> Sats 11 am and 2.30 pm   Suns 2.30pm
> also school holidays
> Box Office   071-836-3344
> # ALADDIN
> 26 November – 22 January
> *From the team that brought you* BEAUTY AND THE BEAST *and* PINOCCHIO *by Andy Rashleigh*

Listening

2 🔲 Listen to this conversation. Where do they decide to go? When?

3 Listen again and complete these sentences.

  a Hello, _____ Carol, please?

  b We _____ Lisa's party.

  c I hope _____ you.

  d Would _____ movie?

  e I think _____ movie.

  f There's _____ the Odeon.

  g I'll _____ seven thirty.

  h Can _____ friend?

Writing

4 Write a letter to someone you don't know, describing yourself and your interests.

> *Dear Box 4789,*
>
> *I'm writing in response to your 'Lonely Hearts' advertisement. I am . . . .*
> . . . .
> . . . .
> . . . .
> . . . .
>
> *Looking forward to hearing from you.*
>
> *Yours sincerely,*

11

Check your grammar
Present continuous

1 Look at these sentences.

  a I'm doing a course in computer graphics.
  b I'm watching TV.
  c I'm not doing anything on Saturday.

Which sentence is about:

  1 something happening at this moment?
  2 something happening these days?
  3 something happening in the future?

Like

2 Translate these sentences into your language.

  a Do you look like your brother?
  b Do you like your brother?
  c What's he like?
  d What does he like?
  e What would he like?

Build your Vocabulary
Negative prefixes

1 Use *un-* or *in-* to make these adjectives negative.

happy – *unhappy*

sensitive	convenient
expensive	friendly
caring	interesting
attractive	married
comfortable	

Relationships

2 What one word can you use to complete all these sentences?

  a I _____ Alex but he doesn't _____ me.
  b Would you like to see a movie? I'd _____ to.
  c They met and fell in _____.
  d We both _____ dancing.
  e I like Kim but we're not in _____.
  f Give my _____ to your mother.
  g There's a new film on at the Odeon. It's a good film – it's a _____ story.

Practise your pronunciation
Word linking

1 📼 How many words do you hear? (Contractions like 'doesn't' count as two words).

Contractions

2 Practise saying this traditional children's poem.

He loves me.
    He don't.
He'll leave me.
    He won't.
He would
    If he could
But he can't
    So he don't.

Now, can you correct the grammar ?
(There are two mistakes).

Unit 12 What's the matter?

1 What's the matter with them? What happened?

2 What do you think they should / shouldn't do?

3 Have you ever had a black eye? Have you ever broken your arm or your leg? Have you ever had an operation? Ask other students.

12

LANGUAGE ACTIVITIES

▶ *Could*
▶ Past simple
▶ Continuous: present and past

1 What could happen?

Why are these activities dangerous? What could happen?

a skiing   *You could fall and break your leg.*
b horseriding
c windsurfing
d bungee jumping
e crossing the road
f cooking

Think of other dangerous activities and say what could happen.

> ◣ *Could* ▶ 13
> You **could** break your leg.

2 Put this conversation in order.

a I was skiing and I fell.
b Yes, much better, thanks.
c Did it hurt?
d What happened?
e Are you feeling better now?
f How did it happen?
g I broke my arm.
h You bet.

3 Write similar conversations for two of the people in Starting Points.

> ◣ **Past continuous and past simple** ▶ 8
> I **was** ski**ing** and I **fell**

4 How are they feeling?

a

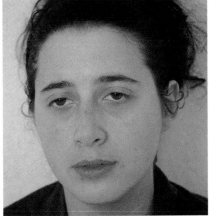

b

c

d

e

f

Ask other students:

How are you feeling?
Why?/What's the matter?

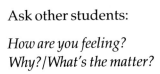

Continuous tenses ▶ 6, 8
How **are** you feel**ing**?
What **were** you do**ing**?

Role play

5 Student A: You are the doctor. Ask Student B questions and give him/her some advice.

Student B: Tell the doctor about your problem.

6 What were you doing? Ask other students.

What were you doing at eight o'clock yesterday evening?
I was watching TV.
What are you doing now?
I'm …

Who was doing the same thing as you?

7 Ask other students about people in their family.

What's your brother doing now?
I don't know. Sleeping, probably.

Pre-reading

1 Look at these pictures. What is happening? Describe one of the pictures to another student.

a

b

c

d

Reading

2 Read these poems written by children. Can you match the poem with the picture?

When I am lonely

When I am lonely
and my brother
will not play with me,
I feel like
the last petal
left on a flower
and the other petals
are floating away.

(Victoria Evans, 6)

When I am happy

When I am happy
I am a proud tree,
still and straight,
covered in green leaves.

(Keeley Oakley, 5)

My Granny

My granny died.
They let her body
stay in the house.
My mammy went to see her
and she brought me.
When she seen my granny
she started to cry.
But me. Just sitting
on a seat, reading my book
not crying at all.

(Dominic McLarnon, 7)

Dancing

My gran came to the school disco
And danced.
In a blue dress she danced.
My granpa was holding her hand in the air.
My gran was laughing when she danced.

(Emma Labross, 6)

Word search

3 Find these words in the poem.

Find two words for 'grandmother' and one word for 'mother'.

Speaking

4 Which poem do you like best? Why? Tell other students.

I like the first poem because …

Pre-listening

5 Make a story about an accident using four of these words.

bottle   bike   tooth   foot
beach   dog   window hospital

Listening

6 🔊 Listen to these people describing accidents they had and decide which picture goes with each story.

7 Listen again and complete the chart.

	Place	Circumstances	Event	Result
1		*running into the sea*		
2				*I was really angry*
3	*in the country*			

105

Illnesses

1 Combine words from Column 1 and 2, or 2 and 3, to make illnesses.

	1	2	3
a	pain in my	back	-ache
	sore	head	
	bad	throat	
	broken	stomach	
		tooth	
		shoulder	
		chest	
		arm	
		leg	
		cough	

a pain in my chest
a broken arm
a headache

Feelings

2 Give advice to these people.

I'm feeling tired.
You should go to bed.

a I'm feeling hungry.
b I'm feeling cold.
c I'm feeling ill.
d I'm feeling sad.
e I'm feeling thirsty.
f I'm feeling angry.
g I'm feeling hot.

Accidents

3 Complete the sentences using one of these verbs. Put the verb in the correct tense.

run into	fall over
cut	fall off
catch	run over
burn	break

a I was riding a horse and I _____.
b I was skiing and I _____.
c I was driving and I _____ a bus.
d I was riding my bike and I _____ a dog.
e I was playing football and I _____ my glasses.
f I was chopping onions and I _____ myself.
g I was lighting the fire and I _____ myself.
h I was walking in the rain and I _____ a cold.

Could ▶13

4 Complete the sentences, saying what could happen:

Don't drink the water.
It could be dirty. You could get sick.

1 Don't play with that knife.
  You _____
2 Take an umbrella.
  It _____
3 Don't drive fast.
  You _____
4 Don't eat that fish.
  It _____
5 Take your sunglasses.
  It _____
6 Don't swim in the river.
  You _____
7 Phone the restaurant.
  It _____
8 Take a sweater.
  It _____

Past simple + past continuous ▶ 8

5 Put the verbs in the correct tense.

I had a bad day yesterday. In the morning I (make) _____
breakfast and I (burn) _____ myself. Then I (drive) _____ to
work and I (run) _____ over a cat. In the office I (work) _____
and the telephone (ring) _____. It was my daughter. She was in
hospital. 'I (play) _____ football and I (break) _____ my arm'.
I (drive) _____ to the hospital and the car (stop) _____ : no
petrol. I phoned my wife. But she (have) _____ a bath. I had
to walk to the hospital. I (walk) _____ to the hospital and it
(start) _____ to rain. I (catch) _____ a bad cold. Today I
think I'll stay in bed.

6 Tell this story.

Continuous tenses ▶ 8

7 Make questions using the correct tense:

this time last year?   *What were you doing this time last year?*

a this time yesterday?
b at 10pm last night?
c now?
d a year ago?
e this time last week?
f an hour ago?
g at 8 o'clock this morning?
h at this very moment?

8 Now, answer the questions in Activity 7.

This time last year I was studying, probably.

SKILLS: LISTENING AND WRITING

Pre-listening

1 What are these things? What are they for?

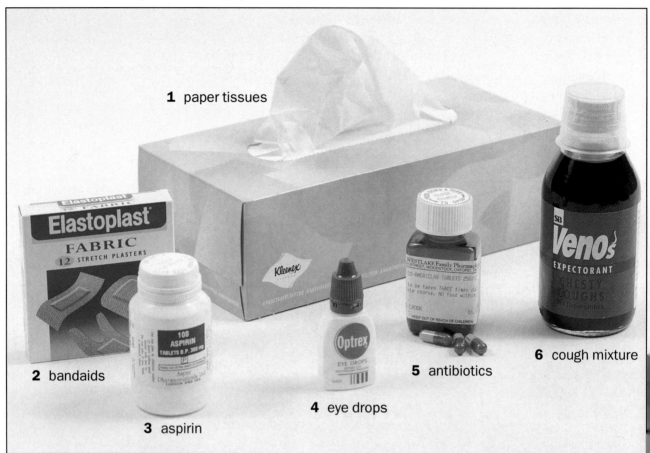

1 paper tissues

2 bandaids

3 aspirin

4 eye drops

5 antibiotics

6 cough mixture

Listening

2 🔊 Listen to these short conversations and fill in the chart.

	Problem	Solution
1		
2		
3		
4		

3 Listen again, and complete these sentences.

a _____ for sore eyes?
b These eyedrops _____ .
c _____ a bad cough?
d I can't _____ in English.
e _____ a tooth infection. What _____?
f I'll take the aspirins. How _____?

Writing

4 Write about an accident that happened to you. Include:

Place: *This happened to me when I was in …*
Circumstances: *I was …ing …*
Event: *… suddenly …*
Result: *I had to … I felt …*

Check your grammar
Continuous

Complete with the correct auxiliary verbs:

a I _____ working at the moment.
b I _____ working yesterday morning.
c _____ you working now?
d _____ you working yesterday?

Could or *should*?

a 'I've got a toothache.' 'You _____ see a dentist.'
b Don't drive fast. You _____ have an accident.
c He's got a bad cough. He _____ n't smoke.
d Be careful with that knife! You _____ cut yourself.

Build your Vocabulary
Word field: Parts of the body

Add more words to these lists:

Head	Body
eye	arm
nose	leg
mouth	

Irregular plurals

What are the plurals of these nouns?

foot
tooth
knife
child
man
woman

Practise your pronunciation
Rhythm

1 🔲 Listen and mark the beats:

What were you doing when it
  started to rain?
When it started to rain?
When it started to rain?
When it started to rain I was
  thinking.

What were you doing when
  you fell off the train?
When I fell off the train?
When I fell off the train?
When I fell off the train I was
  drinking.

2 Practise saying the rhythm.

109

Grammar Reference

These pages give more detailed grammatical explanations, and include reference material for points you need to know at this level.

1   Imperatives

Form: Stand up.
Sit down.

Don't sit down.
Don't write.

Use: For giving instructions and directions.

2   Be

Form: 1 Present

I **am**.
He/she/it **is**.
We/you/they **are**.
Is she? I**'m not**.   They **aren't**.

2 Past

I/He/she/it **was**.
We/you/they **were**.
Was she?   They **weren't**.

Use: 1 For names, jobs, nationalities, ages etc:

It's Korean.
Are you an actor?
I'm 19.

2 To say where things are:

Where is the clock?
It's on the wall.
Derek was at home.

3 With adjectives, for description:

It's cheap.
The food was nice.

3   Have

Form: 1 As main verb

I/you/we/they **have**.
He/she/it **has**.

Do you **have**?   Does it **have**?
She doesn't **have**. We don't **have**.

2 As auxiliary verb

I/you/we/they **have** been/got.
He/she/it **has** been/got.

Have you been? **Has** it got?
She **hasn't** been.   We **haven't** got.

Use: 1 *Have* is a main verb, meaning *possess*:

*We **have** three children.*
*How much money **do** you **have**?*

2 *Have* is an auxiliary verb in the present perfect, and with *got*:

***Have** you seen the new Almodóvar film?*
*He **hasn't got** a car.*

4   Auxiliary verbs: do/does; did; will

Form: 1 Present simple

Do you/I/we/they work?
Does he/she/it work?
I/you/we/they **don't** work.
He/she/it **doesn't** work.

2 Past simple

Did you/I/he/she/it/we/they work?
I/you/he/she/it/we/they **didn't** work.

3 Future simple

Will you/I/he/she/it/we/they work?
I/you/he/she/it/we/they **won't** work.

Use: 1 To make questions:

***Did** you watch TV yesterday?*
*When **do** you have breakfast?*
***Will** you buy a newspaper tomorrow?*

2 To make negatives:

*My sister **doesn't** cook.*
*Robin **didn't** go to Scotland.*

5   Present simple

Form: I/you/we/they **work**.
He/she/it **works**.

Do you work? **Does** it work?
I **don't** work. It **doesn't** work.

Use: 1 For states/facts:

*I **live** in Reading.*
*I **don't eat** meat.*

2 For routines/habits:

***Do** you **watch** TV every day?*
*When **do** you **have** breakfast?*

*I **go** to the gym on Thursday evenings.*
*What time **do you get up**?*

Present continuous

Form: I **am** writ**ing**.
You/we/they **are** writ**ing**.
He/she/it **is** writ**ing**.

Are they writ**ing**? **Is** she writ**ing**?
They **aren't** writ**ing**. She **isn't** writ**ing**.

Use: 1 For an event happening at the moment of speaking:

*What **are you doing**?*
*I'**m writing** a letter.*
*How **are you feeling**?*

2 For a future arrangement, eg when making excuses:

*What **are you doing** on Friday?*
*I'**m not doing** anything on Saturday.*

Past simple

Form: 1 Regular verbs

I/you/he/she/it/we/they **worked**.
Did it work? They **didn't** work.

Irregular verbs

I/you/he/she/it/we/they **went**.
Did she go? We **didn't** go.

Use: For a finished event in the past:

*Jon **stayed** in a youth hostel.*
*Robin **didn't go** to Scotland.*

8 Past continuous

Form: I/he/she/it **was working**.
We/you/they **were working**.

Was he working? **Were** they working?
I **wasn't** working. They **weren't** working.

Use: For describing the background to past events:

*What **were** you **doing**?*
*I **was skiing** and I fell.*

9 Present perfect

Form: I/you/we/they **have been**.
He/she/it **has been**.

Have they been? **Has** she been?
We **haven't** been. He **hasn't** been.

Use: For recent events (exact time not specified):

***Have** you **seen** the new Almodóvar film?*
*No, I **haven't**.*

10 Have got

Form: I/you/we/they **have got.**
He/she/it **has got.**

Have they got? **Has** she got?
We **haven't** got. He **hasn't** got.

Use: 1 To talk about possessions (= *have*):

***Have you got** a pen?*
*He **hasn't got** a car.*

2 For describing people, places:

*The flat **has got** two bedrooms.*
*She'**s got** brown eyes.*

Note: The past of *have got* is *had*:
*The house **had** two bedrooms.*

11 Going to

Form: I **am going to** leave.
He/she/it **is going to** leave.
We/you/they **are going to** leave.

Is he going to leave? **Are they going to** leave?

She's **not going to** leave. (Or: She **isn't going to** leave).
They **aren't going to** leave.

Use: To talk about plans, intentions:

*What **is** she **going to** do?*
*She's **going to** study.*

12   Can/can't

Form: I/you/he/she/it/we/they **can** drive.

Can they drive?
She **can't** drive.

Use: 1 to express ability:

*I **can** read Italian but I **can't** write it.*

2 to make requests:

Can you say that again?
Can you pass me that folder, please?

13   Could

Form: I/you/he/she/it/we/they **could** go.

Could they go?
She **couldn't** go.

Use: to talk about what is possible:

*You **could** break your leg.*

14   Should

Form: I/you/he/she/it/we/they **should** go.

Should they go?
She **shouldn't** go.

Use: to give advice:

*You **should** see this film.*

15   Have to

Form: I/you/we/they **have to** go.
He/she/it **has to** go.

Do you have to go? **Does** she have to go?
We **don't** have to go. He **doesn't** have to go.

Use: To talk about obligations:

*Jason **has to** cross the sea.*
*You **have to** escape.*

16   Would

Form: I/you/he/she/it/we/they **would** like.

Would you like?
I **would** like.

Use: To make offers, invitations:

Would you like a drink?
Would you like some paella?

17   There is/are; there was/were

Use: to describe places, events:

There's a small garden.
There were a lot of people at the football.

18   Like

Form: 1 as verb

I/you/we/they **like** football.
He/she **likes** football.

Do you **like**? She doesn't **like**.

2 as preposition

She looks **like** her sister.
They look **like** a couple.

Use: 1 as verb plus noun or -*ing*, to talk about likes and dislikes.

*Libby **likes** playing tennis.*
*I don't **like** jazz.*

2 as preposition plus noun, to describe things or people:

*Do you look **like** your sister? No, I don't.*
*What's it **like**? It's nice.*
*What's the kitchen **like**? It's modern.*

19   Well

Form: *Well* is an adjective in 'I am very well'. It is an adverb in 'I can speak French well'.

Use: As an adverb, put *well* at the end of the sentence. Use *quite* or *very* for different degrees of ability.

*She can play the piano **well**.*
*I can read French quite **well**.*
*I can't write it very **well**.*

20 Indefinite article: a/an

Forms: Use **a** before consonant sounds. Use **an** before vowel sounds.

a doctor **a** lawyer **a** university student
an engineer **an** hour

Use: 1 To talk about a thing for the first time:

*Jane has got **a** new car.*

2 To say what somebody's job is:

*He's **an** engineer.*

21 Definite article: the

Use: 1 Use **the** when it is clear which person/thing you are referring to:

*I've got two children: a boy and a girl. **The** boy's name is Robin …*
*It is **the** only cinema in **the** centre of town.*
*I'm going to **the** supermarket.*

2 Use **the** for musical instruments:

*Can you play **the** piano?*

22 No

Use: *No* goes with nouns:

*There's **no** garage.*
*We've got **no** money.*

23 Some

Use: *Some* goes with plural countable nouns and uncountable nouns:

*Would you like **some** biscuits?*
*Would you like **some** icecream?*

(But: *Would you like **a** banana?*)

24 Any

Use: Use *any* in questions and negative sentences for an indefinite quantity:

*Have you got **any** children?*
*We don't have **any** sugar.*

25 A lot of

Use: Use with countable and uncountable nouns, in statements, negatives and questions:

*Istvan eats **a lot of** fruit.*
*Zoltan doesn't eat **a lot of** meat.*
*Have you got **a lot of** money?*

26 This/that; these; those

Forms: **This** and **that** are singular.
These and **those** are plural.

This hotel is cheap.
Those students are late.

Use: Use **this** and **these** to refer to things or people near you. Use **that** and **those** to refer to things or people away from you:

*Can you pass me **that** folder?*
***This** folder?*

27 How much? how many?

Use: Use **how much** for uncountable things, and **how many** for countable things:

***How much** sugar do you take?*
***How many** sandwiches would you like?*

28 Which?

Use: Use **which?** for identifying one of a number things:

Can you pass me that folder?
***Which** folder? This blue folder or this green folder?*

29 Whose?

Use: To ask about possession:

Whose guitar is it?
It's Libby's.

30 Wh question words

Form: When, where, what, why, how etc.

Use: Wh-word + verb 'to be' + subject
or Wh-word + auxiliary verb + subject +
main verb
(W + A + S + V)

Where is the clock?
What does Richard do?
How do you go to work?
When did you have breakfast?

31 Adjectives

Form: Adjectives come before nouns or after the
verb **to be**. They have no plural form.

It's cheap.
It's a Swiss watch.
The black cars are taxis.

32 Nationalities

Form:

Country	Adjective	Person
Australia	Australian	an Australian
Brazil	Brazilian	a Brazilian
Canada	Canadian	a Canadian
China	Chinese	a Chinese
Denmark	Danish	a Dane
Egypt	Egyptian	an Egyptian
England	English	an Englishman/woman
France	French	a Frenchman/woman
Germany	German	a German
Greece	Greek	a Greek
Holland	Dutch	a Dutchman/woman
Hungary	Hungarian	a Hungarian
Ireland	Irish	an Irishman/woman
Italy	Italian	an Italian
Japan	Japanese	a Japanese
Korea	Korean	a Korean
Mexico	Mexican	a Mexican
Portugal	Portuguese	a Portuguese
Scotland	Scottish	a Scot
Spain	Spanish	a Spaniard
Sweden	Swedish	a Swede
Switzerland	Swiss	a Swiss
Turkey	Turkish	a Turk
Wales	Welsh	a Welshman/woman

33 Comparatives

Form: Short adjectives:

long ▶ longer
cold ▶ colder
big ▶ bigger
happy ▶ happier

Irregular:

good ▶ better

Long adjectives:

expensive ▶ more expensive
interesting ▶ more interesting

Use: For comparing two things:

*This house is **nicer** than that house.*
*This house is **more expensive**.*

34 Superlatives

Form: Short adjectives:

long ▶ the longest
cold ▶ the coldest
big ▶ the biggest
happy ▶ the happiest

Irregular:

good ▶ the best

Long adjectives:

expensive ▶ the most expensive
intestesting ▶ the most interesting

Use: For comparing one thing in a group with all the others in the group:

*What's **the best** bookshop in town?*

35 Possessive adjectives

Form:

Subject pronoun	Possessive adjective
I	my
you	your
he	his
she	her
it	its
we	our
they	their

Use: Use possessive adjectives with nouns.

*This is **my** car.*
*Is that **your** pen?*

36 Possessive 's

Form: To show possession. Add **'s** after singular nouns.

Use: *Whose guitar is it?*
*It's **Libby's**.*
*This is **Josh's** computer.*

37 Prepositions of time

Form: **at, in, on, from, to** + noun

Use: ***at** six o'clock; **at** 2.15pm*
***in** June; **in** 1992*
***on** Monday*
***from** six o'clock **to** seven o'clock*

38 Prepositions of place

Form: **in, on, under, between, near in front of, beside** etc. + noun

Use: *The book is **under** the table.*
*The clock is **on** the wall.*

39 Impersonal you

Use: 1 Use the imperative or impersonal *you* + verb when giving directions:

*How do **you get** to the station?*
***Go** down this street.*
*Then **you cross** the square.*

2 Use impersonal *you* when talking generally:

***You** buy stamps at a post office.*
(= people buy stamps at a post office)

40 So

Use: Use *so* in expressions like:

*Do you think they are French? I think **so**.*
(= I think they are French)
*I don't think **so**. (= I don't think they are French)*

41 List of Irregular Verbs

Infinitive	Past simple	Past participle	Infinitive	Past simple	Past participle
be	was/were	been	leave	left	left
begin	began	begun	lie	lay	lain
bite	bit	bitten	lose	lost	lost
break	broke	broken	make	made	made
bring	brought	brought	meet	met	met
burn	burnt	burnt	pay	paid	paid
buy	bought	bought	put	put	put
catch	caught	caught	read	read	read
choose	chose	chosen	ride	rode	ridden
come	came	come	run	ran	run
cost	cost	cost	say	said	said
cut	cut	cut	see	saw	seen
do	did	done	sell	sold	sold
draw	drew	drawn	send	sent	sent
drink	drank	drunk	shoot	shot	shot
drive	drove	driven	show	showed	shown
eat	ate	eaten	shut	shut	shut
fall	fell	fallen	sing	sang	sung
feel	felt	felt	sit	sat	sat
fight	fought	fought	sleep	slept	slept
find	found	found	speak	spoke	spoken
fly	flew	flown	spend	spent	spent
forget	forgot	forgotten	stand	stood	stood
get	got	got	steal	stole	stolen
give	gave	given	swim	swam	swum
go	went	gone	take	took	taken
have	had	had	teach	taught	taught
hear	heard	heard	tell	told	told
hide	hid	hidden	think	thought	thought
hit	hit	hit	throw	threw	thrown
hold	held	held	understand	understood	understood
hurt	hurt	hurt	wake	woke	woken
keep	kept	kept	wear	wore	worn
know	knew	known	win	won	won
learn	learnt/ed	learnt/ed	write	wrote	written

INDEX

Thematic Word List

Classroom (Unit 1)

video 1
cassette 1
board 1
chair 1
table 1
book 1
pen 1
teacher 1
student 1
bag 1
clock 1
window 1
door 1
wall 1

Prepositions of place (Unit 1)

in 2
on 2
under 2
behind 2
in front of 2
next to 2
near 2
between 2

Action verbs (Unit 1

go 4
find 3
walk 5
stop 4
sit down 2
stand up 4
open 3
turn 3
point 2
touch 5
put 7

Parts of body (Unit 1)

head 5
eye 5
ear 5
mouth 5
nose 5
arm 5
hand 5
finger 5
back 5
stomach 5
leg 5
foot 5
toe 5

Personal possessions (Unit 1)

key 8
calculator 8
diary 8
wallet 8
comb 8
business card 8
credit card 8
sunglasses 8

Colours (Unit 2)

blue 9
white 9
red 9
green 9
yellow 9
black 9

Nationalities (Unit 2)

Japanese 10
Korean 10
Italian 14
Portuguese 14
Russian 14
Chinese 14
Brazilian 14
Swiss 10
English 13
Greek 14
Spanish 14
Swedish 14
Hungarian 14
Turkish 14
Canadian 11
Australian 14
Irish 14
Egyptian 14
Indian 13
American 11

Consumer durables (Unit 2)

car 14
radio 17
computer 14
watch 10

Jobs (Unit 2)

student 11
doctor 14
teacher 14
actor 14
secretary 14
sales assistant 14

mechanic 14
librarian 13
professor 14
bank clerk 14
fireman 10
writer 13
football player 15
social worker 15

Places (Unit 2)

office 14
shop 14
library 14
bank 14
hospital 14
university 14
theatre 14
school 14
garage 14

Stationery (Unit 2)

dictionary 16
notebook 16
battery 16

Personal information (Unit 2)

name 14
age 16
nationality 14
occupation 11
marital status 13
married 11
single 11
divorced 12
birthday 10
address 11
telephone number 16

Family (Unit 3)

grandmother 18
grandfather 18
father 18
mother 18
wife 18
husband 18
sister 18
brother 18
son 18
daughter 18
uncle 18
aunt 18
children 18
parent 18
cousin 18
twin 19
baby 26

119

windsurfing 60
sightseeing 65
cycling 65
climbing 60

Housing (Unit 8)

house 68
flat 68
block of flats 69
skyscraper 71
tent 71
furnished 69
bedroom 68
bathroom 70
kitchen 68
living room 68
garage 70
garden 68
balcony 67
dining room 69

Furniture (Unit 8)

armchair 70
sofa 70
bed 70
bath 70
shower 70
toilet 69
bookcase 70
cooker 70
fridge 70
microwave 70
wardrobe 70

Description (Unit 8)

wide 73
narrow 73
fast 71
slow 71
low 73
high 73
new 73
old 73
good 73
bad 73
attractive 73
comfortable 73
expensive 73
cheap 73

Geography (Unit 9)

mountain 75
island 79
cave 79
lake 79
river 79
forest 79
sea 79

city 79
jungle 75
ruins 75

Action verbs (Unit 9)

get lost 79
lose 79
find 79
meet 79
escape 79
chase 79
arrive 83
return 83
rescue 75

Prepositions of movement (Unit 9)

over 81
through 81
up 81
down 81
round 81

Shops and amenities (Unit 10)

bookshop 85
newsagents 89
pharmacy 89
supermarket 89
cinema 89
restaurant 89
coffee shop 89
music shop 89
post office 88
station 90
bus stop 92

Two-part verbs (Unit 10)

get out 89
try on 89
take out 89
get on 89
get off 89

Character and appearance (Unit 11)

friendly 96
handsome 96
caring 96
slim 96
loving 96
warm 96
well-built 96
sensitive 96

Relationships (Unit 11)

separated 96
widowed 98
engaged 98

Nationalities (Unit 11)

a Finn 98
an Italian 98
a Pole 98
a Spaniard 98
a Brazilian 98
a Turk 98
a Swede 98
a German 98
a Greek 98
a Swiss 98
a Portuguese 98
an Englisman/woman 98

Illnesses (Unit 12)

a bad cold 106
a broken arm 101
a toothache 106
a headache 106
a bad back 106
a black eye 101
a cough 106
a sore throat 106
a pain 106

Sensations (Unit 12)

tired 106
hungry 106
cold 106
ill 106
sad 106
thirsty 106
angry 106
hot 106

Accidents (Unit 12)

run into 106
cut 106
catch 106
burn 106
fall down 106
fall off 106
run over 106
break 106